D1053089

Peer-to-Peer Video Streaming

Peer-to-Peer Video Streaming

Eric Setton

Streaming Media Systems Group
Hewlett-Packard Laboratories
Palo Alto, CA

Bernd Girod

Information Systems Laboratory
Department of Electrical Engineering
Stanford University
Stanford, CA

 Springer

Eric Setton
Streaming Media Systems Group
Hewelett-Packard Laboratories
Palo Alto, CA 94304
eric.setton@hp.com

Bernd Girod
Information Systems Laboratory
Department of Electrical Engineering
Stanford, CA 94305
bgirod@stanford.edu

ISBN-13: 978-0-387-74114-7   e-ISBN-13: 978-0-387-74115-4

Library of Congress Control Number: 2007932753

To my parents
Eric Setton

Preface

Live video broadcasting over the Internet requires an infrastructure capable of supporting a large number of simultaneous unicast connections. Since the costs of providing this service grow with the number of viewers, television networks have been reluctant to offer it to their customers on a large scale. Peer-to-peer architectures are an alternative where viewers contribute their resources to the network to act as relays, hence overcoming the need for a dedicated content delivery infrastructure.

Peer-to-peer video streaming systems offer the same advantages as peer-to-peer file transfer networks but face additional challenges since data transfer needs to occur continuously to avoid playout interruptions. This is particularly difficult since the peers are connected to the Internet by links which may have different capacity and reliability. Moreover, data delivery paths may simply disappear without prior notice, e.g., when a peer leaves the broadcast. This challenging environment is a perfect field of application for recent advances in compression, streaming, and networking and a catalyst for new progress. Remarkably, functioning solutions have emerged and the research community now expects that in the future peer-to-peer video streaming system will be used for large-scale live television distribution over the Internet.

One of the goals of this book is to provide an overview of today's state-of-the-art peer-to-peer video streaming technology and to show how it can be improved in terms of video quality, robustness, and latency. We present adaptive video coding and streaming techniques which enhance the performance of conventional client-server systems and extend them to peer-to-peer multicast. We focus on throughput-limited environments where congestion often hampers interactivity and fast response times. We analyze the benefits of scheduling packet transmissions and retransmissions in a way which adapts to the particular properties of video streams and to the changing topology of peer-to-peer networks. The performance of the solutions we propose is assessed by analyzing the results of experiments carried out over simulated networks with large numbers of peers.

The contents of this book is the result of research carried out over the course of the last few years at Stanford University. The text itself is based on the 2006 Ph.D. dissertation of the first author. Compared to this original work, the presentation has been revised substantially and additional material of interest has been added.

The authors would like to thank the members of the Image, Video and Multimedia Systems group at Stanford and the members of the Streaming Media Systems group at HP Labs for many insightful discussions. We are grateful to John Apostolopoulos for his continuous support and his many helpful comments and to Jeonghun Noh for his work on the peer-to-peer control protocol. Amy Brais and Jennifer Evans, at Springer, were very supportive and provided us with a lot of assistance.

Palo Alto, CA, USA   *Eric Setton*
                                                      Bernd Girod

Contents

1

Introduction

Since the appearance of Napster in early 1999, peer-to-peer (P2P) networks have experienced tremendous growth. In 2003, P2P became the most popular Web application, and, at the end of 2004, P2P protocols represented over 60% of the total Internet traffic, dwarfing Web browsing, the second most popular application [1]. This rapid success was fueled by file transfer networks which allow users to swap media files, despite the large latency often necessary to complete a download. It is expected to continue at a fast pace, as new compelling P2P applications are developed. One of these applications, P2P multicast, is explored in this book.

In P2P multicast, a media stream is sent to a large audience by taking advantage of the uplink capability of the viewers to forward data. Similar to file transfer networks, data propagation is accomplished, via a distributed protocol, which lets peers self-organize into distribution trees or meshes. The striking difference is that this should happen in real-time, to provide all connected users with a TV-like viewing experience. Compared to content delivery networks, this approach is appealing as it does not require any dedicated infrastructure and is self-scaling as the resources of the network increase with the number of users.

To become widely adopted, P2P streaming systems should achieve high and constant video quality, as well as low startup latency. Three factors make this a difficult task. First, the access bandwidth of the peers is often insufficient to support high quality video. Second, the peers may choose to disconnect at any time breaking data distribution paths. This creates a highly unreliable and dynamic network fabric. Third, unlike in client-server systems, packets often need to be relayed along long multi-hop paths, each hop introducing additional delay, especially when links are congested. This unique set of challenges explain why early implementations, although they constitute remarkable progress and demonstrate the feasibility of large scale P2P streaming, fall short of the goals.

In our own research, which is presented in this book, we have investigated video streaming systems in order to enhance the perceived image quality, increase their robustness to errors, and reduce latency. As the techniques that we are considering have merit for both client-server and P2P networks, our approach is to analyze the performance of unicast systems first, before extending and adapting the algorithms to P2P multicast. We investigate, in particular, throughput-limited environments where video streams may cause self-congestion when their rate is too high or when their transmission is inadequately controlled. In this context, we show the importance of adaptive packet scheduling which may help extend the range of sustainable rates, reduce startup latency, and maintain high error resilience.

The rest of this book is organized as follows. In the next chapter, we describe recent advances in the field of video compression, video streaming, multicast architectures and P2P systems, related to our work. In Chapter 3, we consider client-server systems. We focus on the impact of self-inflicted congestion on low-latency video streaming. We present an end-to-end rate-distortion model which captures the impact of both compression and late loss due to self-inflicted congestion. The model is helpful for deriving an encoding rate which maximizes video quality. In the second part of the chapter, we introduce the concept of congestion-distortion optimized (CoDiO) packet scheduling. Different from rate-distortion optimization, this type of algorithm determines which packets to send, and when, to maximize decoded video quality while limiting network congestion. We describe the operations of this scheduler, and of a low-complexity scheduler derived from it, and analyze their performance over a simulated network. The experimental results presented in this chapter are the first in-depth comparison of congestion and rate-distortion optimized schedulers.

In Chapter 4 and in Chapter 5, we consider the scenario of live P2P multicast where the video stream is sent to a large population of peers. Before showing how adaptive streaming algorithms can be adapted to this context, we describe a distributed control protocol, designed for fast startup, which is run by the peers to construct and maintain multiple multicast trees rooted at the video source. This allows to transmit a video stream synchronously to a set of peers by relying on their forwarding capacity. The operations of this protocol are described in detail and an analysis of its performance over different networks is presented. In Chapter 5, we explain how to extend congestion-distortion optimized packet scheduling to P2P live streaming to further reduce startup latency and to support higher rates. Similar to the CoDiO scheduler, the adaptive scheduler we present transmits in priority packets which contribute most to the decoded video quality. In addition, it favors peers which serve, subsequently, larger populations since they have the largest impact on the overall video quality. This one-to-many packet scheduler is combined with a retransmission scheduler which operates at the receivers to request, in priority, missing packets which will lead to the largest distortion reduction. We investigate the performance of this streaming technique over simulated networks of hundreds of peers. Conclusions and future research directions are presented in Chapter 6. The appendix contains additional technical details about the different video streaming experiments reported previously in the book.

2

Background

The purpose of the work presented in this book is to analyze and improve the performance of video streaming systems operating in bandwidth-constrained networks. In particular, we consider low-latency applications where a source is serving a single receiver or where video is multicast to a population of peers. Our work builds upon recent advances which have focused on providing better compression efficiency, on increasing the robustness of video streaming systems, and on building efficient multicast architectures or peer-to-peer systems. In the following, we present an overview of the state-of-the-art in these areas.

2.1 Video Compression

2.1.1 H.264 Video Coding

The results we present in the following chapters were obtained for video sequences compressed using the latest video coding standard H.264, also called MPEG-4 Advanced Video Coding or H.264/AVC, which was finalized in March 2003 [2]. Like its predecessors, H.261, MPEG-1, H.262 (MPEG-2), H.263 and MPEG-4 [3, 4, 5, 6, 7], H.264 is a hybrid codec which combines blockwise transform coding and motion-compensated predictive coding to reduce the redundancy of a video signal. Overviews of modern video coding and in particular of H.264 can be found in [8, 9, 10, 11]. Two technically similar video coding standards, Microsoft's SMPTE VC-1 and the Chinese Advanced Video coding Standard AVS, are presented in [12, 13] and in [14]. Compared to H.263, H.264 achieves bit rate reductions of up to 50% at a comparable quality. This gain is the result of a combination of new features introduced in the standard: these include better motion-compensated prediction with multiple reference frames and varying block sizes down to 4x4 pixels [15], spatial prediction of intra-coded blocks, and improved entropy coding [16]. A reference software implementation of H.264 has been made freely available [17].

The standard specifies three major profiles: the *Baseline* profile which is mindful of the computational complexity, the *Main* profile, designed to take full advantage of the coding efficiency of H.264, and the *Extended* profile, which includes a number of enhancements for streaming applications [18]. Recent additions to the standard include an extension for higher fidelity (e.g., 10 bits/sample) video signals called FRExt (Fidelity Range Extension) [19] and an extension for Scalable Video Coding (SVC) [20, 21].

The basic components of a hybrid video encoder are shown in Fig. 2.1. The input video signal is predicted from previously transmitted information available both at the encoder and the decoder, and the prediction error is compressed, typically with a transform coder operating on a block-by-block basis. The prediction can be based on information in other frames ("motion-compensated predictor") or in the same frame ("intra predictor"). As in still picture coding, intra-prediction exploits correlation among adjacent pixels in the image. More specific to video is motion-compensated prediction that uses one or several previously encoded frames as references to predict the current frame. Depending on the type of prediction allowed, we distinguish three types of coded frames: Intra (I) frames do not use temporal prediction but only intra-prediction; Predicted (P) frames use only one previously encoded frame as a reference; Bi-directionally predicted (B) frames combine prediction from two reference frames[1]. In general, I frames produce a much larger bit rate than P frames. The best coding efficiency can be achieved by using B frames. The residual signal after prediction is transformed in the frequency domain and quantized. Finally, entropy coding techniques, like context-based variable length coding or arithmetic coding, are applied to compress the syntax elements representing the video signal, which include motion vectors, coding modes, and quantized transform coefficients.

Higher compression efficiency makes the signal more susceptible to transmission errors. Even the corruption of a single bit in the compressed stream may preclude the decoding of a video syntax element and, since context-based entropy coding is used, such an error will affect all the following syntax elements until a re-synchronization marker is encountered. In addition, error propagation may occur within a frame, when a corrupted pixel value is used for prediction of adjacent pixels. Finally, regions of an image that cannot be correctly decoded create artifacts that are propagated over several consecutive frames, due to temporal prediction. Error propagation will continue until the next I frame is successfully decoded, since this type of picture does not depend on previously encoded pictures.

---

[1] Please note that these restrictions are required in MPEG-1 and MPEG-2. The most recent H.264/AVC standard is much more general and allows but does not mandate I, P, and B frames as described here.

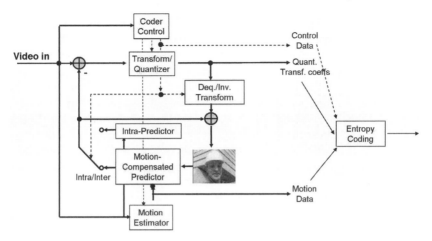

Fig. 2.1. Diagram of a motion-compensated hybrid video coder according to H.261, MPEG-1, MPEG-2, H.263, MPEG-4, or H.264/AVC standards. The intra-inter switch controls whether spatial or temporal prediction is used for compression. Dependency between frames is introduced via the motion-compensated inter-frame prediction when P frames and B frames are encoded.

2.1.2 Distortion Models

Performance of Motion-Compensated Video Coding

To study the performance of hybrid video coding, a theoretical framework is developed in [22]. An analysis of the rate-distortion efficiency of motion-compensated coding is presented in this paper, where a closed-form expression is obtained by assuming the different image signals and motion-compensated predictors are stationary and jointly Gaussian zero-mean signals. Hence, the resulting rate-distortion function can be thought of as an upper bound to the rate-distortion function for a non-Gaussian image signal with the same power spectral density. Although this is a simplification, the model has been widely used in the literature to evaluate the performance of several image or video encoders. The performance of I frames and P frames is derived for integer-pixel and fractional-pixel motion accuracy in [22] and studied further in [23]. The rate-distortion efficiency of B frames can be obtained from the model extension to multi-hypothesis predictive coding proposed in [24]. Other extensions are presented in [25, 26, 27] where the effect of the size of the set of predictors and of the correlation between the different predictors is analyzed. In [28] and [29], the authors show that the model can also be helpful to quantify the performance of scalable video codecs.

Empirical Distortion Models

The model described in [22] is general and well-suited to gain insight on the influence of different elements composing a video coding system. However it assumes ideal compression performance and, as such, does not reflect the performance of specific implementations of video codecs. This has motivated research on more practical distortion models which are obtained by analyzing the empirical performance of various codecs, as in [30] for example.

In [31], a model is proposed to characterize the rate-distortion performance of H.263 video streaming with P frames. This includes an analysis of the encoder distortion and of the impact of transmission errors on the decoded signal. Despite its simplicity, this model accurately predicts end-to-end performance. In this book, we show that the use of this model can be applied to a video stream encoded with H.264, and can be extended to a video streaming system operating in a throughput-limited environment. More complex models have also been proposed to account more accurately for the impact of packet loss. Many focus on the error propagation which occurs, due to predictive-video coding, when part of an image has to be concealed by the decoder [32, 33, 34]. Other models capturing the influence of specific loss patterns are studied in [35] and [36]. They have been employed to enhance the performance of video streaming systems, which are reviewed in the following section.

2.2 Video Streaming

Multimedia applications have experienced explosive growth in the last decade and have become a pervasive application over the Internet. Despite the growth in availability of broadband technology, and progress in video compression, the quality of video streaming systems is still not on par with SDTV and even further from HDTV. This is due to the best-effort nature of the network which does not offer any guaranteed quality of service (QoS) and where bandwidth, delay and losses may vary unexpectedly. The advent of wireless last hops, and the emergence of multi-hop ad hoc networks bring as additional challenges interference, shadowing and mobility. It is a daunting task to achieve high and constant quality video, and low startup delays and end-to-end latencies, in such environments. Recent overviews and special issues reviewing progress in video streaming can be found in [37, 38, 39, 40] and in [41, 42, 43] for the case of wireless networks. In the following we focus on advances related to error resilience, congestion control and multi-path delivery.

2.2.1 Error Resilience

Error control techniques help mitigate the impact of transmission errors or of packet loss on the quality of the decoded video [44, 45]. They are essential to applications for which it is difficult to achieve timely and error-free delivery of the stream. Examples include interactive applications that require low latencies, e.g. two-way video communications, Internet-based television, etc., or situations where the network fabric is unreliable, as in the case of peer-to-peer applications or of wireless links. For such applications, it is well known that the separation principle of source and channel coding put forth in Shannon's information theoretic work does not hold, as it would require infinite length codewords and large delays. Hence, joint source and channel coding techniques have been proposed, but have not yet lead to a unified solution to this problem, as explained in [46]. These considerations, however, have strongly influenced the video coding community in the design of a highly flexible network-friendly syntax in H.264 [47]. It has also motivated the networking community to consider different prioritization classes for traffic with varying QoS requirement [48, 49].

Robust Video Coding

One approach to error control is to increase the robustness of the bitstream produced by video encoders by increasing the redundancy at the cost of lower coding efficiency. This can be done, for example, by varying the amount of intra-coded pictures, slices or macroblocks in the compressed video, which can be decoded regardless of the state of the decoding buffer as they do not rely on information carried by other parts of the bitstream [50, 51, 31, 52]. More generally, it is possible to incorporate, at the encoder, the effect of loss in the mode decision process to minimize the expected distortion. This principle governs the reference picture selection (RPS) algorithm [46], adopted as an extension of H.263, which adapts the encoding to feedback information sent by the decoder. These algorithms are investigated and extended in [53, 54, 55, 56, 57]. Similar ideas can also be applied to pre-stored bitstreams and do not require the use of a live encoder [58, 59, 60].

Forward Error Correction

The performance of a video streaming system can also be improved by protecting the encoded bitstream with channel coding. One of the most popular ways of achieving this is to apply forward error correction (FEC) across the different packets of a compressed video stream, notably with Reed Solomon codes. In this way a receiver can recover the encoded stream from any large enough subset of packets. For video streaming, the priority encoding transmission (PET) scheme proposed in [61] is a popular way to provide unequal error protection (UEP) of different layers of a scalable video representation [62, 63, 64]. Optimizing the bit-rate and the amount of protection of the different layers is studied in [65, 66, 67, 68]. FEC can also be combined with data partitioning which separates the stream into different segments and prioritizes important information such as headers and motion vectors [69] or to protect a region of interest using in particular the new error resiliency tools provided by H.264 such as flexible macroblock ordering (FMO) [70, 71].

Rate-Distortion Optimized Scheduling

The FEC-based approach outlined above is most efficient when the loss statistics are known at the sender. In many cases however, losses occur in bursts or their statistics are time-varying. Hence, in practical streaming systems, the most common error control technique is Automatic Repeat reQuest (ARQ) where lost packets are recovered through retransmission [72, 73, 74]. ARQ systems use combinations of time-outs and positive and negative acknowledgments to determine which packets should be retransmitted. Unlike FEC schemes, ARQ automatically adapts to varying channel loss rates and, hence, tends to be more efficient for the Internet. Advanced schemes can allow for prioritized retransmission of more important packets. This leads to the general question of finding the best schedule of transmissions and retransmissions of a packetized media stream. One of the earliest publications that addresses in a rigorous manner the issue of scheduling transmissions and retransmissions of layered media representations is the 1998 technical report on Soft ARQ [75] which introduces a Markov chain analysis to find the optimal transmission policy. Unfortunately, a search space growing exponentially with the number of packets considered for transmission limits the practicality of the solution. In a related paper, Miao and Ortega suggest a low-complexity heuristic for the problem [76].

A particularly intriguing framework for computing rate-distortion optimized packet scheduling policies has been developed, at around the same time, by Chou and Miao [77, 78]. We will refer to their framework and its various extensions as RaDiO throughout this book. Like [75], RaDiO considers the unequal importance of packets. Its aim is to find an optimal schedule which minimizes the Lagrangian cost $D + \lambda R$, where D represents the expected distortion and R is the average transmission rate. The algorithm considers consecutive time slots in which each packet can potentially be transmitted and optimizes the schedules of different packets iteratively until convergence. The complexity is reduced by considering a limited time horizon, and optimized policies are recomputed, at each new time step, taking into account feedback. RaDiO has been extended by Kalman et al. to include the impact of error concealment that better reflects the properties of video streams [79]. Its performance has been studied for different configurations by Chakareski et al., notably for server-driven and receiver-driven scenarios [80, 81].

A particular challenge of the RaDiO framework is its computational complexity. As noted in [82], optimization is NP-hard and can be cast as a variation of the classic knapsack problem. In addition, Röder et al. show that the iterative descent algorithm suggested by Chou and Miao does not always guarantee good solutions [82]. As an alternative, low-complexity schemes based on the formulation of Chou and Miao have been proposed [83, 84]. Another serious limitation is that the work in this area has usually considered vastly over-provisioned networks where the impact of the transmitted stream itself on end-to-end delay can be neglected. Although the performance of RaDiO has sometimes been studied in simulations replicating delay patterns and losses collected from the Internet [85, 84] or for time-varying statistics [86, 87], the case of scheduling the media stream over a throughput-limited network, prone to congestion, which we address in this work has not been investigated in depth.

Error Concealment

When losses cannot be avoided, error concealment is used at the decoder as the last line of defense. The most common technique is that of simple frame repetition, which requires no additional computation but does not correct visual artifacts. Temporal linear interpolation algorithms can also be easily implemented at the decoder to create new frames. They create significant ghosting artifacts in the case of large displacements. More advanced schemes have been proposed based on a combination of spatial and temporal motion-compensated interpolation. These techniques estimate motion and create an image by displacing objects (e.g., pixels or macroblocks) along computed trajectories [88, 89, 90, 91].

2.2.2 Congestion Control

When bandwidth is limited, congestion control algorithms are needed to allocate a fair share of the network path's throughput to a video streaming application. Some commercial applications use multiple-file switching to offer a choice between video streams compressed at different bit rates [92]. Another simple alternative is to let TCP regulate the communication at the transport layer [93]. However, because of the resulting fluctuating throughput due to its *additive increase and multiplicative decrease* behavior, this method is not well suited to low-latency applications and causes frequent buffer underruns at the receiver. Therefore, congestion control schemes such as TCP-Friendly Rate Control (TFRC) [94] or other equation-based rate control algorithms [95], which smooth out the sudden rate variations of TCP, have been considered to estimate for the streaming system a suitable transmission rate. In the case of wireless channels, other throughput estimators are often employed as it is important to differentiate between losses due to congestion or to corruption on the wireless medium [96, 97, 98, 99].

The rate derived by the transport layer is relayed to the application layer which adapts accordingly. In live encoding systems, a control mechanism is used to adjust the quantization and modulate the size of the stream produced by the encoder [100, 101, 102, 103, 104, 105]. For pre-encoded video, throughput can be adapted by discarding successive layers of a scalable representation as in [106, 107] and in [108, 109] for the case of a scalable H.264 bitstream. For a single-layered coding scheme, transcoding the stream allows to reduce the bitrate and bypass the computational overhead of re-encoding. Such techniques are reviewed in [110]. Another possibility is to use H.264 SP frames to switch between different quality streams [111, 112, 113]. In this book, we consider single-layer encoding. The goal of our content-adaptive scheduler is to determine an optimal tradeoff between congestion created over the network and decoded video quality, by selecting the most important portions of the video to transmit in priority.

2.2.3 Path Diversity

Path diversity at the network layer can also help improve the overall performance of a streaming system. A sender may, for example, select the best end-to-end network path in terms of bandwidth, losses, or delay, or distribute a media stream along different routes.

On the Internet, as today's routers do not support source routing between two end hosts, path diversity can be obtained, for example, by means of an overlay of relay nodes [114, 115]. When losses are correlated, splitting video packets between different independent routes is a way to protect the bitstream from consecutive losses, which can have dramatic impact on decoded video quality [35]. This technique is often combined with multiple description coding to send independently decodable streams over different paths [115, 116, 117, 118, 119, 120]. When the probability of simultaneous losses on the paths is low, the error resilience increases at the cost of lower compression efficiency. For video coding, multiple descriptions can be obtained by temporal or spatial sampling e.g. [121, 122], or by using different transforms and quantizers [123, 124, 125, 126, 127]. When feedback is available, the sender can also simply decide to switch to a more reliable route when burst losses are detected [57, 59]. Another approach is to use an optimized algorithm, such as RaDiO, to perform both path selection and packet scheduling [87, 128, 129, 130].

Different systems have been proposed to combine the resources of multiple servers or of multiple peers to achieve higher throughput. In [131, 132], a video client determines how to allocate rate between several throughput-limited forwarders to maximize received video quality. In addition, losses over the different paths can be mitigated by protecting the streams with FEC in a synchronized fashion [118, 133, 134]. Distributing video traffic along different routes also has merit in the case of wireless ad hoc networks as long as interference along concurrent paths is limited. This idea has been investigated to achieve higher aggregate throughput in [135, 136] or to provide redundancy when mobility causes a path to fail as in [137, 138]. In these cases, the statistics are monitored periodically and new paths are sometimes necessary to adapt the routing to the network conditions or to node mobility.

In the work we present, we take advantage of multi-path streaming since different peers are used to transmit complementary portions of a video stream. The peer-to-peer architecture presented in Chapter 4 and in Chapter 5 leverages diversity for error resilience by requesting packet retransmissions over alternate paths.

2.3 Multicast Architectures

The aim of the P2P video streaming system we analyze in Chapters 4 and 5 is to distribute a video stream synchronously (i.e., multicast) to a large population of viewers. In this section, we review alternative architectures designed for video multicast which do not use P2P networks.

2.3.1 IP Multicast

In IP multicast systems, a source transmits a single stream which is replicated by the routers of the network to achieve one-to-many distribution. This system, initially proposed by Deering [139], lets different receivers access the stream by subscribing to the corresponding multicast group maintained by the routers. Although this architecture is elegant as it places minimal burden on the network resources, multicast is not universally deployed and is not available outside proprietary networks or research networks such as Mbone.

A question for multicast systems, in general, is how to find an equivalent to the adaptability of unicast systems [140, 141]. This is particularly important in the case of bandwidth heterogeneity. To protect networks from feedback implosion, techniques which do not rely on acknowledgments, or end-to-end signalling, have been designed and go beyond the simple approach of satisfying the requirement of the receiver with the worst performance limitations. Such systems may rely on layered video coding where the base layer and each of the enhancement layer form different multicast streams which a user can subscribe to. Determination of the optimal number of layers is performed by the client, which can adjust this parameter if its available throughput varies [142].

To provide reliability to multicast video transmission, some authors have suggested to employ retransmission requests in the event of packet loss as mentioned in [143]. Such feedback-based schemes need to be made scalable in the multicast context which assumes forming groups of receivers and some kind of priority or hierarchy to limit the bandwidth on the back channel as in [144]. If the loss rate can be estimated accurately, full reliability can be achieved even in the case of losses, through FEC [145, 146]. UEP techniques, mentioned above for the server-client scenario, have also been extended to IP multicast [147].

2.3.2 Content Delivery Networks

Today, one-to-many commercial streaming solutions are offered via content delivery networks (CDNs), such as Akamai, Limelight or VitalStream [148, 149, 150]. They are based on an overlay of replication or mirror servers, to which users are redirected when the maximum number of streams of an individual media server (typically between a few hundred and a few thousand) is exceeded. The design issues and performance evaluation of one of these leading networks is described in detail in [151].

As the number of mirror servers increases, the scalability of the system grows as a larger user base can be supported. In addition, it becomes easier to offer some guarantees in terms of content availability or robustness to losses. Understanding and improving the tradeoffs between the cost of the system and these performance improvements is the focus of research on content replication algorithms which indicate how many mirror servers are needed and where they should be placed [152, 153, 154, 155].

When the content distributed by the overlay is a live media stream, dynamic algorithms are employed to adapt, in real-time, to the varying number of users and to their location. Protocols run by the different overlay nodes create a distribution tree between the broadcast source and the different overlay nodes [156, 157, 158]. This tree can approach the efficiency of IP multicast when the overlay nodes form a dense enough set of edge servers.

2.4 Peer-to-Peer Systems

Peer-to-peer (P2P) systems are a special type of overlay network where there is little or no dedicated infrastructure and the peers, or clients, act as potential forwarders and, more generally, contribute their resources to the system [159]. This concept has many applications which range from grid computing, to distributed storage or, as considered in this book, real-time media delivery. Today's most popular systems are mostly driven by media file sharing. The most popular ones, e.g., eDonkey and BitTorrent (or any client running these protocols) have millions of users and represent a large portion of Internet traffic [1]. One of these clients, eMule, has reportedly been downloaded over 300 million times as of April 2007, which makes it the most successful open source project to date [160]. In these systems, different peers coordinate to download files, without requiring costly webservers to host and transmit content. The distributed nature of these systems require specific protocols to locate, store or download content, and has fostered a large amount of research and development in both the academic and open source communities. All these goals are shared by P2P streaming systems which incorporate, in addition, a latency constraint. In this section, we give an overview of the widely deployed BitTorrent protocol, describe recent advances in the area of P2P file sharing protocols, and finally focus on P2P streaming systems which will be a central topic of this book.

2.4.1 Peer-to-Peer File Transfer, the Example of BitTorrent

BitTorrent is an open source protocol [161] which was created in 2001 by Bram Cohen, to overcome the shortcomings of prior P2P systems. In particular, BitTorrent aims at fully utilizing the uplink throughput of peers which have downloaded or are downloading a particular file. The main characteristics of the BitTorrent protocol include:

- Dividing files into small chunks of data, which can be downloaded by a peer independently of each other, and providing a simple system to check the integrity of each chunk.
- Incorporating simple uploading rules in the clients to enhance the performance of the system in terms of download speed, and of lifetime of a file in the P2P network. These include downloading the rarest chunk first and reciprocation, i.e., "tit-for-tat" uploading.

The original BitTorrent system was successful at creating a large community of users, moderated by some active members, in charge of inspecting each new file in the P2P system, in order to maintain high quality and avoid pollution.

A BitTorrent system is composed of four parts. The first component is the *seed*, a user who has a complete copy of a file she wishes to share with other peers. The second component is the *.torrent* file. This file is created by a seed and published on a regular webserver. It contains enough metadata to describe the file: the number of chunks into which data is separated and the SHA-1 [162] signature of each chunk, used to verify the integrity of the file, as it is being downloaded. In addition, it also indicates the address of a *tracker*. Trackers are the third component of BitTorrent systems. They are hosts which continuously monitor the download of the file by storing the addresses of the different peers which have downloaded or are downloading the file, as well as some additional information reflecting their performance. Finally, the fourth component are the actual *peer nodes*. The peers initially access the .torrent file, register with the corresponding tracker, and use it to obtain a list of connected peers. They locate missing chunks of the file by exchanging their buffer map with other active peers. These maps indicate the chunks they hold and the ones they are missing. Uploads and downloads between peers are negotiated following rules which we describe in the next paragraph. Periodically, peers report their download status to the tracker of the .torrent file. A detailed description of the syntax and implementation of the BitTorrent protocol has been made available to the public [161], and has resulted in a flurry of BitTorrent compliant clients, which compete on the quality of their content, of their client, and of their community. Some of these, notably, include Azureus, utorrent, ABC, TurboBT, BitComet, as well as the original BitTorrent client.

Once a BitTorrent client has obtained a list of active peers from the tracker, it locates different chunks of the file by exchanging its buffer map (initially empty) with the other members of the session. It then requests the rarest chunks from the peers which hold them. This strategy decreases the likelihood that a torrent will die as a consequence of one of the chunks disappearing from the network. This, obviously, would preclude any download from completing. Peers serve a small number of incoming requests simultaneously (typically 4). The speed at which the chunks are uploaded is dictated by TCP. When choosing among different requests, priority is given to requests from peers which themselves have provided chunks previously. This prioritization is known as the "tit-for-tat" rule. A small number of connections (typically 1) is also reserved for serving peers, regardless of the amount of data these peers have provided in the past. This is particularly advantageous for peers which have recently joined and which have not yet been able to provide any data. The motivation for this altruistic "optimistic unchoking" rule is that it may result in establishing a high-speed connection to a new peer which may be worthwhile in the future, as a consequence of tit-for-tat. Finally, when almost all the pieces have been downloaded, a peer will try to get the same remaining chunks from multiple peers at once to avoid being held up by a peer with a slow connection.

The emergence of large P2P file transfer systems with large amount of users and traffic has enabled researchers to investigate and attempt to model user behavior [163, 164], or to study the evolution of large distributed systems, e.g., [165, 166]. Several improvements to systems like BitTorrent have also been proposed, e.g., [167, 168, 169].

In one particularly interesting direction one tries to avoid any centralized index whatsoever. In the case of Napster, a centralized index was used to hold a list associating the files present on the network to the address of computers. In BitTorrent, a centralized list of peers is held by the tracker. The lack of any centralized index (largely motivated by piracy) creates an interesting challenge in terms of content discovery. A significant amount of work has addressed the problem of how to locate a file among a large set of users given its name and the IP addresses of a very limited set of connected peers. Beyond the simpler flooding approach [167], proposed solutions rely on distributed hash tables (DHT) which map a key, representing a file, to a value, indicating a peer, and are distributed among the users. As each peer only maintains a small part of the table, the algorithms also indicate how queries can be conducted on the whole table efficiently, through message exchanges. Such systems, including the popular Chord, CAN, and Pastry, are analyzed in [170, 171, 172, 173, 174, 175], where their scalability, efficiency and resilience are examined.

The BitTorrent protocol has proven to be very reliable as a result of its simplicity. One of its main characteristics is that it is data-driven. Peers look for particular pieces of data, regardless of the peers which hold them. This differs from other approaches where clients try to identify peers which hold the data and establish lasting connections to them, as, for example, in Kazaa, one of BitTorrent predecessors. This data-driven approach avoids the need of precisely measuring the amount of available throughput of different peers and monitoring the different connections. This distinction between data-driven protocols and connection-driven protocols, or, as these approaches are also referred to, between un-structured and structured systems [176] also exists in P2P video streaming systems.

2.4.2 Peer-to-Peer Streaming

In P2P streaming systems, a critical requirement is to operate the media distribution continuously. Hence, the difficulty resides not only in *content* location, but also in *resource* location, as peers need to discover which other connected hosts have enough throughput to act as forwarders and relay the media stream they have received. To the best of our knowledge, one of the earliest proposals for this type of system is by Sheu et al. [177], which focuses on building a distributed video-on-demand system for ATM networks. More recent work on P2P asynchronous video streaming can be found in [178, 179, 180, 181], and a good deployment example is the P2P client Joost, which improved the progressive download feature originally incorporated in Kazaa, to offer on-demand viewing of pre-recorded television shows.

The concept of live P2P multicast was made popular by Chu et al. [182] who suggested taking advantage of the resources of the users to form a dynamic delivery network which would offer the same viewing experience as live television. The idea is appealing as it does not require any infrastructure and is, in theory, self-scaling, as the number of peer *servers* and peer *clients* increase at the same rate. Even though this field is still in its early stages, it has become, in the last few years, a very active area of research. Many proposed systems rely on distributed protocols to construct one or several multicast trees between the media source and the different users to distribute the stream [183, 184, 185, 186]. Another approach lets peers self-organize in a mesh and request different portions of the video from their neighbors, with no particular emphasis on the structure of the distribution path [187, 188, 189]. Along with these early research experiments, many applications have appeared on the Internet, such as PPLive, PPStream, TVU networks, Zattoo, etc. One of the main goals of these applications is to enable the largest possible set of users to connect to each other by integrating to their protocol Network Address Translator (NAT) and firewall traversal techniques. These problems have been partially resolved via protocols which employ third-party rendez-vous servers [190, 191, 192, 193, 194]. All these implementations constitute very exciting progress and demonstrate the feasibility of large-scale P2P streaming. As an example, both PPLive and Gridmedia [188] have been reported to support over 100,000 peers simultaneously with a small number of servers. However all these systems typically suffer from long startup delays (possibly on the order of minutes) and often cannot sustain constant video quality.

In the second half of the book, we study a live P2P streaming system, based on a protocol which constructs and maintains multiple multicast trees. We analyze the unique issues of video transport over P2P networks, and notably consider the impact of multimedia packet scheduling on the overall performance, focusing especially on low latency. We show that to achieve better performance in P2P video streaming systems, application-layer multicast and video transport should be considered jointly. The closest work that we know of is that reported in [195] and in [196, 197], which associate separate layers or video descriptions with different application-layer multicast trees and FEC for robustness. This differs from our approach which is based on distortion-optimized techniques for scheduling of transmissions and retransmissions of a single-layer stream.

3

Streaming over Throughput-Limited Paths

Streaming real-time media might increase the congestion of bottleneck links. This may disrupt the transmissions of other users and even delay the delivery of the media stream itself. In the first part of this chapter, we analyze the impact of self-congestion on the performance of a low-latency media streaming system operating over a throughput-limited network path. We present a rate-distortion model which captures both the effect of compression and of late losses due to congestion on the decoded video quality of the system. This model is helpful to determine how close to the physical channel capacity a low-latency video streaming system can operate.

In the second part of the chapter, we present the concept of congestion-distortion optimized (CoDiO) streaming. This is one of the main contributions of this book. Our work builds on the RaDiO scheduling framework, which considers unequal contributions of different portions of a multimedia data stream to the overall distortion. Rather than searching for an optimal schedule for the packets of a stream, which minimizes the expected Lagrangian cost of rate and distortion, we suggest changing metric and replacing rate by congestion, which we define, throughout this book, as expected end-to-end delay. We explain why congestion is better suited to throughput-limited streaming, and describe how, given a simple channel model, CoDiO scheduling is performed. We also present a low-complexity version of our algorithm, CoDiO light, simple enough to run in real-time. Experimental results analyze the performance of CoDiO and CoDiO light compared to a content-oblivious ARQ scheduler. We also analyze how our congestion-distortion schedulers compare to the state-of-the-art RaDiO scheduler.

3.1 Video Encoding for Throughput-Limited Paths

In this section, we present a model to estimate the highest sustainable rate, given a fixed encoding structure, for a video streaming system operating at low latency over a throughput-limited network path.

3.1.1 End-to-End Rate-Distortion Performance Model

In low-latency streaming applications, compressed video is transmitted over a network at a given rate. Typically, it is desirable to achieve end-to-end delays of no more than a few hundred milliseconds. When a packet does not arrive at the receiver by its playout deadline, to avoid interruptions, the decoder conceals the missing information and the playout continues at the cost of higher distortion. Decoded video quality at the receiver is therefore affected by two factors: quantization errors introduced at the encoder while compressing the media stream, and packet loss either caused by transmission errors or due to late arrivals. These two contributions have different characteristics. Typically, the distortion introduced by quantization is evenly distributed across the encoded frames and is determined by the encoding bit-rate. This contrasts with the impact of packet loss which usually introduces decoding errors (i.e., higher distortion) in the frame(s) containing the missing packet(s). Because of the predictive nature of the compressed video stream, this error will propagate to subsequent frames. Usually, these errors tend to decay over time due to intra-macroblock coding and in-loop filtering. Error propagation is eventually stopped when an intra-coded frame is received. Using Mean Square Error (MSE) as the criterion, a video distortion model can be derived based on [31][1]. The decoded video distortion, denoted by D_{dec}, comprises two terms:

$$D_{dec} = D_{enc} + D_{loss}, \qquad (3.1)$$

where the distortion for the encoder performance D_{enc} and the contribution from packet loss D_{loss} are described in greater detail in the following.

Encoder Distortion Model

The distortion introduced by encoder quantization is reduced when the sequence is encoded at a higher rate. As the coding rate increases, however, the same amount of distortion reduction requires a greater rate increment. In [31], this distortion-rate tradeoff is modeled for H.263 P frame encoding, by a simple formula:

$$D_{enc} = D_0 + \Theta/(R - R_0), \qquad (3.2)$$

where R is the rate of the video stream, and D_0, Θ and R_0 are model parameters. Using nonlinear regression techniques, these parameters can be estimated from empirical rate-distortion curves obtained by encoding a sequence at different rates. Interestingly, we have observed that this model can also be extended to sequences encoded by H.264, with more complicated GOPs, incorporating I, B, P pictures as well as SP and SI pictures [135, 198, 199]. In

---

[1] Part of the derivation presented in this section is reproduced with permission from [198] © 2004 IEEE and from [135] © 2005 Elsevier.

this case, the parameters D_0, Θ and R_0 need to be estimated for the specific GOP structure considered. As an illustration, Fig. 3.2 shows the model fit for six CIF sequences, encoded by H.264 for the GOP structure shown in Fig. 3.1. Please note that the same GOP structure will be used for all the experimental results presented in this chapter. More details on the peak-signal-to-noise-ratio (PSNR) metric used to measure video quality and on the sequences can be found in Appendix A.

Fig. 3.1. Group of pictures and their encoding structure. The first picture of the group is an I frame, it is encoded using intra-prediction only. Differential coding is used to compress P frames and B frames. P frames are encoded after forming a motion-compensated prediction based on a preceding frame, as depicted by the prediction arrows. B frames are bi-directionally predicted frames, they depend on the neighboring P frames or I frames. This coding structure is periodically repeated to encode the entire video sequence.

Distortion from Loss

The contribution of packet losses to decoded video distortion has been analyzed in detail in [31]. The additional distortion introduced by packet loss depends not only on channel statistics such as packet loss rate, but also on the properties of the encoded sequence such as the percentage of intra-coded macroblocks or the effectiveness of error concealment at the decoder.

Assuming no feedback information and small loss rates, D_{loss} is shown to be linearly related to the frame loss rate P_{loss} as:

$$D_{loss} = \kappa P_{loss}, \tag{3.3}$$

where the scaling factor κ reflects the sensitivity of the encoded video sequence to losses. Figure 3.3 shows how κ is determined experimentally for 6 different sequences. In this experiment, frames are dropped uniformly at random for different loss rates. The resulting decoded distortion is collected and shown in Fig. 3.3. Sequences are encoded by H.264 for the GOP structure shown in Fig. 3.1. They are looped 80 times to obtain stable results. When a frame is lost, previous frame concealment is applied, as explained in Appendix A.

The value of κ indicates the difficulty to conceal losses and reflects the level of activity of the sequences. High activity sequences such as *Foreman* and *Mobile* have higher κ than low activity sequences such as *Mother & Daughter*. Results of additional experiments indicate that κ does not vary much with the encoding rate.

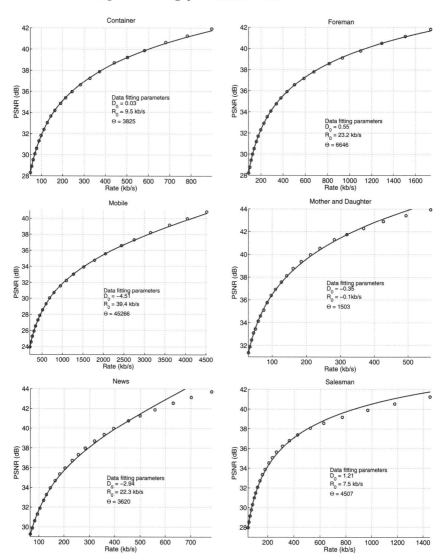

Fig. 3.2. Encoder distortion fit for 6 sequences. Video quality is measured in terms of PSNR, represented in dB and rate is shown in kb/s. The values indicated for the three parameters D_0, R_0 and Θ are used throughout this chapter.

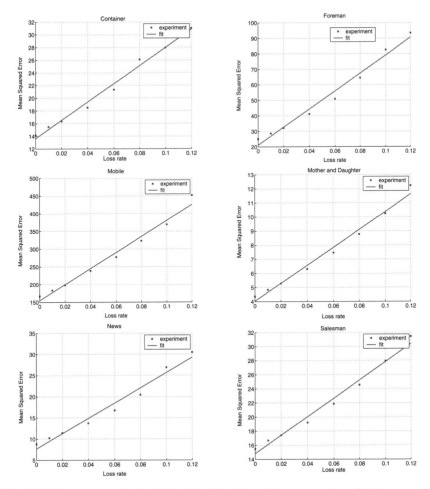

Fig. 3.3. Linear regression to determine the value of the parameter κ for 6 sequences. The encoding rate for the different sequences is as follows. Container: 283 kb/s, Foreman: 290 kb/s, Mobile: 306 kb/s, Mother and Daughter: 319 kb/s, News: 319 kb/s, Salesman: 311 kb/s. The estimated value of κ for the different sequences is as follows. Container: 143, Foreman: 580, Mobile: 2262, Mother and Daughter: 64, News: 180, Salesman: 130.

For low-latency streaming, P_{loss} reflects the combination of random losses and late arrivals of video packets. When the capacity of the network path between the sender and the receiver is limited, we suggest using the M/M/1 queuing model to express this probability. If we consider the channel as a single-hop path and assume the traffic on this link to be exponentially distributed, the late loss probability is expressed:

$$\mathbf{Prob}\{Delay > T\} = e^{-\lambda T}, \tag{3.4}$$

where λ is determined by the average delay:

$$\mathbf{E}\{Delay\} = 1/\lambda = L/(C - R). \tag{3.5}$$

In (3.5), C is the capacity of the link, R is the rate, and L is the packet size. In practice, however, video frames are transmitted at regular intervals over one or several multi-hop paths, the situation is therefore different from that captured by this simple model, where arrivals follow a Poisson process and packets have exponentially distributed service times. Nevertheless, we suggest to model the probability of late loss by an exponential:

$$\mathbf{Prob}\{Delay > T\} = e^{-(C'-R)T/L'}, \tag{3.6}$$

In (3.6), R represents the total transmitted rate; C' is the capacity, i.e., the capacity of the bottleneck in the case of single path transmission, or the aggregate capacity of the paths in the case of multi-path transmission; T is the playout deadlines, this quantity is defined in Appendix A. As traffic does not follow the Poisson distribution, the parameter L' needs to be determined empirically.

We verify that the delay of video packets can be approximated by an exponential distribution and determine the parameter L' by running the following experiment. Video packets are transmitted over a 375 kb/s bottleneck link and their end-to-end delay is collected. Video frames are sent, at regular intervals, 30 times per second, in their encoding order. The sequences are encoded at around 300 kb/s (precise rates for the 6 different sequences are indicated in the caption of Fig. 3.4) and are looped 40 times. The encoding structure is depicted in Fig. 3.1. The empirical frame loss rate for the different sequences is shown for different playout deadlines in Fig. 3.4. The exponential model curve is also shown alongside the empirical results. It follows (3.6), where $C' = 375\ kb/s$, and R is the encoding rate of the different sequences. The value of $L' = 4\ kbit$ is computed by minimizing the mean square error between the model and the empirical curves at the points represented in the figure, for playout deadlines between 250 ms and 900 ms[2]. Results for a similar experiment are shown in Fig. 3.5, for encoding rates of approximately 700 kb/s and a 750 kb/s bottleneck link. In this case, we determine the optimal value $L' = 8\ kbit$, again by minimizing the mean square error between the model and the empirical curves at the points represented in the figure, for playout deadlines between 250 ms and 900 ms. This increase is not surprising as L' reflects the average frame size.

As shown in the figure, the fit between the empirical distribution and the model is acceptable for all the sequences. It is better for the sequence *Mother and Daughter* and worse for the sequence *News*. The shape of the empirical distribution is a consequence of the packet size variation in the video stream. This variation is due to the fact that frames of different types have very different sizes, I frames are 3 to 10 times larger than P frames which, in turn,

---

[2] This is a simple convex optimization problem.

are 2 to 7 times larger than B frames. The variation is also due to frame size increases or decreases which occur when the content of the scene changes or when the motion in the sequence varies. These are particularly noticeable in *Foreman* and in *Mother and Daughter*, as illustrated in Appendix A. Cross traffic is yet another reason for adopting the exponential model, as random arrivals of cross-traffic packets will contribute to increasing the delay spread of video packets. However, experiments show that for cross-traffic rates below 50% of the capacity, and for exponentially distributed cross traffic, the influence of cross traffic on the loss rate is minimal, as long as C' remains constant.

By combining (3.6) with a random frame loss rate P_r, independent of the congestion created over the network, we obtain the overall loss rate:

$$P_{loss} = P_r + (1 - P_r)e^{-(C'-R)T/L'}. \tag{3.7}$$

The total distortion contribution due to packet loss is:

$$D_{loss} = \kappa P_{loss} = \kappa(P_r + (1 - P_r)e^{-(C'-R)T/L'}). \tag{3.8}$$

Total Distortion

The received video distortion can be expressed by regrouping (3.1), (3.2) and (3.8):

$$D_{dec} = D_{enc} + D_{loss}$$
$$D_{dec} = D_0 + \Theta/(R - R_0) + \kappa(P_r + (1 - P_r)e^{-(C'-R)T/L'}). \tag{3.9}$$

The proposed formula models the impact of the rate on the video distortion. Specifically, this model expresses that at lower rates, reconstructed video quality is limited by coarse quantization, whereas at higher rates, the video stream will lead to more network congestion and to longer packet delays, which in turn will cause higher probability of late packets, hence reduced quality. For low-latency video steaming in bandwidth-limited environments, we therefore expect to achieve maximum decoded quality for some intermediate rate.

Optimal Encoding Rate

The optimal encoding rate, R^*, is obtained by setting to zero the derivative of (3.9) with respect to R. This reduces to:

$$\sqrt{\frac{\Theta L}{\kappa T(1 - P_r)}} e^{-(C'-R^*)T/2L'} - R^* + R_0 = 0. \tag{3.10}$$

Although we know of no closed-form solution for (3.10), there is no difficulty in solving this equation numerically.

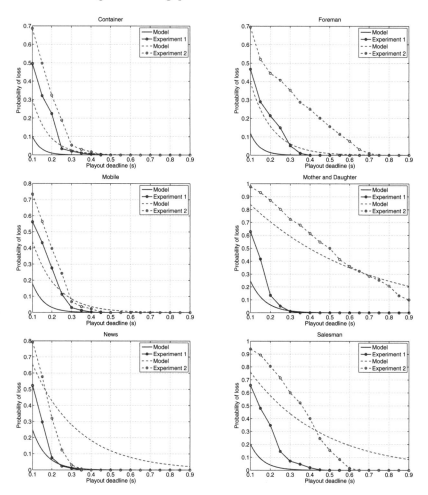

Fig. 3.4. Empirical frame loss rate for different playout deadlines compared to an exponential model for six CIF sequences. The comparison is shown for two different rates. The encoding rate for the different sequences and the different experiments are as follows. Container: 283 kb/s and 327 kb/s, Foreman: 290 kb/s and 338 kb/s, Mobile: 306 kb/s and 342 kb/s, Mother and Daughter: 319 kb/s and 368 kb/s, News: 319 kb/s and 358 kb/s, Salesman: 311 kb/s and 364 kb/s. The bottleneck rate is 375 kb/s.

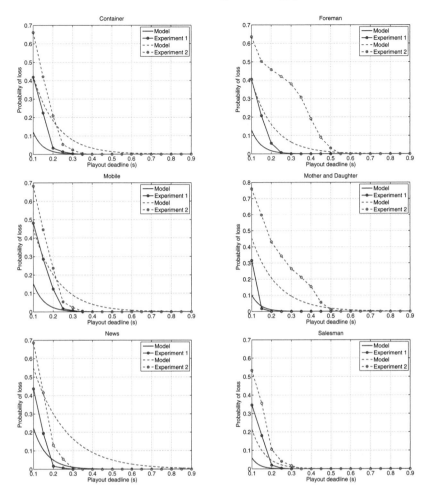

Fig. 3.5. Empirical frame loss rate for different playout deadlines compared to an exponential model for six CIF sequences. The comparison is shown for two different rates. The encoding rate for the different sequences and the different experiments is as follows. Container: 582 kb/s and 682 kb/s, Foreman: 587 kb/s and 677 kb/s, Mobile: 600 kb/s and 686 kb/s, Mother and Daughter: 567 kb/s and 687 kb/s, News: 630 kb/s and 702 kb/s, Salesman: 524 kb/s and 627 kb/s. The bottleneck rate is 750 kb/s.

3.1.2 Experimental Results

In this section, we assess the accuracy of the proposed model by comparing it to experimental results collected over a network simulated in ns-2 [200][3]. In addition, we evaluate the amount of over-provisioning necessary to maximize the end-to-end video quality and analyze how it relates to various parameters.

Experimental Setup

We evaluate the performance of a simple video streaming system as follows. A video stream, encoded with H.264, is sent from a sender to a receiver over a multi-hop path. The total propagation time along the path is very short (i.e., 5 ms). In the first scenario, the capacity of the bottleneck link is 500 kb/s and we consider a low-latency application where packets have just a few hundred milliseconds to reach the receiver or else they are considered lost. In addition to video traffic, the bottleneck link also carries 125 kb/s of cross traffic (one fourth of the link capacity). Cross traffic is specified as a random process, with exponentially distributed packet sizes and arrivals. In this case, the average packet size is 1500 bits, and the average inter-arrival time is 12 ms. We also consider another scenario, with higher throughput, in which the capacity of the bottleneck is 1 Mb/s. The rate of the cross traffic is 250 kb/s (one fourth of the link capacity), with an average packet size of 1500 bits, and an average inter-arrival time of 6 ms.

We collect results for sequences encoded at various rates with H.264. The encoding structure is that shown in Fig. 3.1. The Variable Bit Rate (VBR) encodings are generated by using a constant quantization parameter for I, P and B frames for the whole sequence. Different rates are obtained by varying this quantization parameter. No rate control is used. More detail on the encoded sequences is given in Appendix A.

Video frames are sent, at regular intervals, 30 times per second, in their encoding order. In this set of experiments, there is no retransmission and no feedback from the receiver. We loop the 10-second video clips 60 times to ensure statistically significant results. At the transport layer, the video frames are sent over UDP and encoded frames exceeding the maximum transmission unit (MTU) size of 1500 bytes are fragmented before being sent. When one of these packets is delayed beyond its playout deadline, the frame it belongs to is discarded and we use previous frame concealment until the next decodable picture, as explained in detail in Appendix A.

Analysis

Results for a 500 kb/s bottleneck link and different playout deadlines are shown in Fig. 3.6, along with the fitted model, and in Fig. 3.7 for a 1 Mb/s

---

[3] Please note that, in this book, all the results pertaining to streaming experiments are collected in this simulation environment.

bottleneck. The curves are obtained by first fitting the parameters R_0, D_0, Θ to the rate-distortion curves of the encoded sequences, as shown in Fig. 3.2. The throughput, C', is 375 kb/s and 750 kb/s, respectively (this is obtained by subtracting the rate of cross traffic to the physical capacity of the bottleneck link). κ and L' were determined in the previous section for these values of C'.

While the low rate region of the curve follows closely the encoder rate-PSNR performance as few packets experience excessive delays, there is a sharp degradation when the rate exceeds a certain threshold. This is the region where the bottleneck is overwhelmed, at times, by the video stream. As shown in Fig. 3.6, for a playout deadline of 250 ms, the drop-off occurs at rates well below the physical capacity for all the sequences except for *Mobile*, and similarly, in Fig. 3.7, for a playout deadline of 150 ms, for all the sequences. For longer playout deadlines, i.e., 500 ms and 250 ms, respectively, the drop-off is only observed for 2 of the 6 sequences, namely, for *Foreman* and *Mother and Daughter*. Despite the presence of cross traffic, these results are predicted very accurately by the curves shown in Fig. 3.4 and Fig. 3.5 which indicate, for rates close to capacity, the playout deadline for which losses begin to occur. Depending on the content of the sequence, drop-offs occur for different reasons. For most cases (namely, for *Foreman*, *Mother & Daughter*, *Salesman*, and *News*), losses of one or several I frames occur following a rate increase in the sequence which causes an increase in the queuing delay. For the other two sequences, (namely, *Mobile* and *Container*), the limiting factor is the size of the I frames which limits very low latencies, regardless of the queuing delay. As a reference, rate variations of the different sequences are illustrated in the curves shown in Appendix A.

The curves of the model accurately predict the performance in most of the cases. The differences between the empirical performance and the model are most noticeable for *Mobile* and for *News*. In the first case, the decoded video quality is either excellent (when all the I frames are received) or very bad (when they all miss their decoding deadline), whereas the model always predicts progressive degradations. In the second case, the mismatch is due to the fact that the fit shown in Fig. 3.4 and Fig. 3.5 is not accurate for this sequence. The fit can be improved by reducing the value chosen for L'.

The amount of over-provisioning depends on the playout deadline, on the rate variations of the sequence, and on the bottleneck rate. We present, in the following, an analysis of these effects.

Tighter playout deadlines increase the over-provisioning necessary for a lossless transmission, in other words, effective capacity is reduced by the delay constraint. For example, for a 375 kb/s bottleneck, the highest quality is achieved for *Mother & Daughter* for 319 kb/s when the playout deadline is 500 ms and for 282 kb/s when the playout deadline is 250 ms. In the different cases, this represents 85% and 75 % of the available throughput.

Instantaneous rate increases create queuing spikes at the bottleneck which prevent very low-latency streaming. This explains why the over-provisioning is most noticeable for the two sequences *Foreman* and *Mother & Daughter*. For sequences produced using rate control, where the sizes of each frame are kept close to constant, it is possible to remove the need for over-provisioning. For a bottleneck rate of 375 kb/s, constant bit rate sources can be supported up to 97 % and 99 % of the available throughput for playout deadlines of 250 ms and 500 ms, respectively. However, this performance improvement comes at the cost of fluctuating quality.

For higher bottleneck rates, the amount of over-provisioning necessary is reduced. This is illustrated in the differences between the results shown in Fig. 3.6 and Fig. 3.7 for a playout deadline of 250 ms. For all the sequences except *Foreman* and *Mother & Daughter*, the performance degradation is not observable when the available throughput is 750 kb/s, whereas it is clearly visible for all the sequences except *Mobile* when the available throughput is 375 kb/s. For *Foreman* the peak performance is observed when the rate is 67% of the capacity, for the first experimental setup, and at 77% of the capacity, for the second. For *Mother & Daughter* the peak performance is observed when the rate is 74% of the capacity, for the first case, and at 76% of the capacity, for the second. These results are consistent with the M/M/1 model which predicts that for a given utilization of the link, average queuing delay decreases when the bottleneck rate increases.

Additional results for this model can be found in [135] for an IPP... coding structure. In [135], we also explain that longer groups of pictures make the sequences more sensitive to losses. This increases κ and also increases the need for over-provisioning. This is also the case for the coding structure we consider in this chapter.

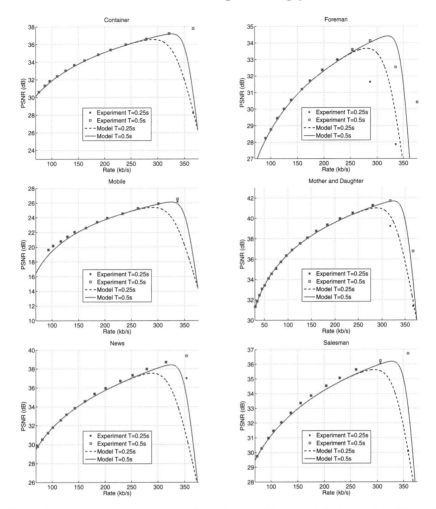

Fig. 3.6. Comparison of the rate-distortion model to empirical data for different playout deadlines. Results shown for 6 sequences. Due to cross traffic, the maximum possible for the video stream is 375 kb/s. Beyond this rate the bottleneck queue grows without bounds.

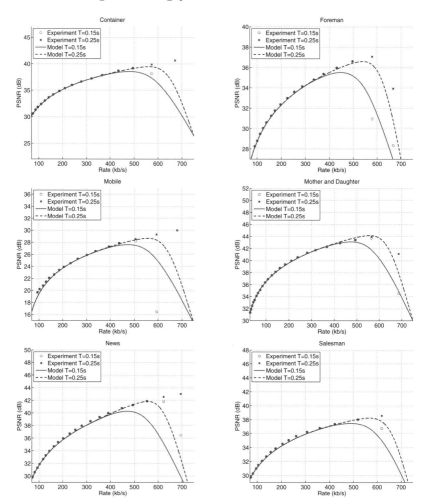

Fig. 3.7. Comparison of the rate-distortion model to empirical data for different playout deadlines. Results shown for 6 sequences. Due to cross traffic, the maximum possible for the video stream is 750 kb/s. Beyond this rate the bottleneck queue grows without bounds. For the sequences *Container* and *Mobile* the decoded video quality for the highest encoding rate is respectively 19 dB and 11 dB. It is not represented on the graphs.

3.2 Congestion-Distortion Optimized Scheduling

The analysis and the model presented in the first part of this chapter show the importance of taking into account the impact of a media stream on the network in terms of congestion. The congestion created by a stream manifests itself as the additional queuing delay which appears on the links carrying its traffic. This effect is not adequately captured when the packet scheduler controls average rate, as in [77, 79, 80]. The same average rate can give rise to vastly different congestion, depending on bottleneck rate and the burstiness of the transmitted stream. This problem has motivated us to develop a new media scheduler based on congestion control instead of rate control. We refer to this new approach as congestion-distortion optimized packet scheduling, or CoDiO.

Different from RaDiO, CoDiO determines which packets to send, and when, to maximize decoded video quality while limiting network congestion. In this section, we analyze the performance of congestion-distortion optimized scheduling for low-latency streaming over a throughput-limited network and compare it to other techniques. We also present a low-complexity algorithm which achieves nearly optimal performance. To our knowledge, and with the exception of our own prior work [201] and [202], the experimental results in this section are the first comparison of congestion-distortion optimized and rate-distortion optimized schedulers.

In Sec. 3.2.1, we describe a time-varying channel model which reflects the impact of a sender on the end-to-end delay of a throughput-limited path. This model takes into account the state of the bottleneck queue and is helpful to estimate the probability that a video packet meets its playout deadline. In Sec. 3.2.2, we explain how to evaluate the congestion created in the network and the expected decoded distortion, given a particular schedule indicating which packets to send, and when, over a finite time horizon. The search space for different possible schedules of a set of packets grows exponentially with the length of the time horizon considered and with the number of packets. This makes it impractical to exhaustively search for an efficient schedule. Besides, coupling between the transmission schedules of different packets prevents scheduling each media packet independently of the others. We present the idea of a randomized schedule search to determine an efficient schedule for the packets of a media stream in Sec. 3.2.3. In Sec. 3.2.4, we also describe a low complexity CoDiO scheduler, which does not require the computational complexity of CoDiO, and adaptively determines which is the next best packet to send to optimize performance. In Sec. 3.2.5, we analyze experimental results which highlight the advantages of CoDiO for low-latency streaming. We also study the benefits of using a congestion-distortion tradeoff instead of a rate-distortion tradeoff. As congestion is an increasing function of the transmission rate, a CoDiO scheduler should achieve similar rate-distortion performance as a RaDiO scheduler. In addition, it is expected to shape traffic to reduce delay over bottleneck links.

Results shown in this chapter are for video streams, transmitted over a wired network, compressed using the encoding structure depicted in Fig. 3.1. The concept of CoDiO scheduling, however, is more general and applies to any type of media encoding and any throughput-limited network. Results for CoDiO scheduling of a layered video representation were presented in [201], and CoDiO scheduling in a time-varying wireless ad hoc network was analyzed in [202].

3.2.1 Channel Model

The channel model we consider is motivated by typical video streaming sessions between media servers and clients, connected to the Internet by a throughput-limited connection susceptible to losses. We consider the route between the video server and the client as a succession of high-bandwidth links, shared by many users, and of a bottleneck last-hop link. The high-bandwidth links are assumed to be lossless. Losses may occur, however, after the bottleneck link. These losses are assumed to be independent, and identically distributed. Different studies have shown that the delay over a multi-hop network path can be well approximated by a shifted gamma distribution, in the absence of congestion, [203, 204]. This is the distribution of a sum of shifted exponential variables and is in agreement with the classic $M/M/1$ model often used to model the distribution of the service time over each network hop [205]. Therefore, in the rest of the chapter, the delay over each link of the first portion of the path will be modeled as a random variable following a shifted exponential distribution (where the shift represents the propagation delay). The delay over the low-bandwidth last hop is determined by the capacity of the link and the size of the queue. The resulting end-to-end delay between the server and the client, as depicted in Fig. 3.8, follows a distribution resulting from the convolution of different exponentials characterizing the delay over each high-bandwidth links, and parameterized by a time-varying shift reflecting the total propagation delay and the delay at the bottleneck. The latter is a consequence of the varying size bottleneck queue, depicted in Fig. 3.9, which can be estimated given the arrival times of packets at the bottleneck, their sizes, and the capacity of the link denoted by C.

The available capacity of the bottleneck link may be estimated by transmitting packets at successive intervals over the network as described, for example, in [206]. For simplicity, we assume that the capacity of this link is known at the sender, that the last hop is not shared with any other streams, and that the bottleneck queue is empty before the streaming session begins. In addition we also assume that the server has an accurate estimate of the parameters of the distributions characterizing the high bandwidth links as in [77, 79, 80]. Given this information and the history of past transmissions, the server may estimate, at each time, a delay distribution, parameterized by the size of the bottleneck queue, and, in turn, the probability that a packet will arrive at the client by a certain time.

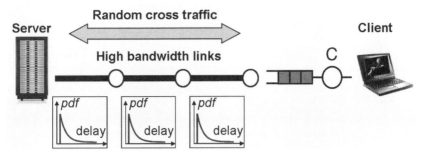

Fig. 3.8. Channel model. The delay over each high bandwidth links is assumed to be exponentially distributed and the delay over the last hop is determined by the size of the bottleneck queue.

3.2.2 Evaluating a Schedule

We consider time to be slotted, and denote by t_j successive transmission times, by δt the length of the time interval between successive transmission times, and by $\pi_i(t_j)$ binary variables representing whether or not the transmission of Packet i of size B_i is scheduled at time t_j. This set of variables for the different times $\{t_1, ..., t_k\}$ is what we define as a *schedule* over k time slots and denote by π. We define as the time horizon the time interval $[t_1, t_1 + k \cdot \delta t]$. In the following we explain how to evaluate the congestion and expected distortion associated with a particular schedule.

Congestion Estimation

Expected end-to-end delay is our metric for congestion and we denote this quantity by Δ. The properties of end-to-end delay make it well-suited to reflect the impact of a sender operating over a throughput-limited network. Unlike the transmission rate, congestion depends on the capacity of the network. As an example, the congestion created on a T3 link when sending 100 kb/s will be much lower than when the same traffic is sent over a 200 kb/s capacity link. As a consequence, congestion also captures changes in the network conditions which may arise when the number of senders competing for network resources changes. The case of time-varying networks, however, studied in our previous work, [202], will not be further addressed in this chapter. Another interesting property of congestion is that it grows without bounds when the transmitted rate approaches the capacity of the bottleneck link. This makes it suitable to evaluate the cost of various transmission schedules and, if used appropriately, should prevent a sender from overwhelming a bottleneck link.

For a given transmission schedule π, the rate output by the server may be used to derive the size of the bottleneck queue as a function of time. This, in turn, leads to an average value of end-to-end delay over the time horizon considered. The transmitted rate at time t_j is:

$$R(t_j) = \sum_i \pi_i(t_j)B_i \qquad (3.11)$$

The additional information needed to derive the size of the bottleneck queue is the time each packet reaches the bottleneck. We assume that delay introduced by the high-bandwidth links can be considered constant and equal to the mean of the actual delay distribution. This approximation is valid when the occupancy of these links is low and the variance created by cross traffic is limited. It is confirmed by the observation that the average utilization of the backbone is well below 30% [207]. As losses occur only *after* the bottleneck and that the bottleneck link is not shared, assuming the delay over the high-bandwidth portion of the network to be equal to its expected value makes the queuing process at the bottleneck deterministic. Therefore, knowing the capacity of the bottleneck link, the transmitted rate as a function of time, and the value of the average delay over the high-bandwidth links, the size of the queue may easily be computed. A typical illustration of the size of the queue as a function of time is shown in Fig. 3.9.

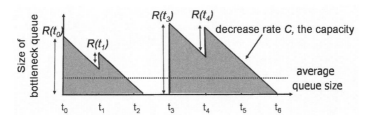

Fig. 3.9. Backlog at the bottleneck queue, as a function of time.

The corresponding average end-to-end delay is simply the average value of this function taken over the time horizon considered and of a constant term which reflects the average delay over the high bandwidth links. In our experiments, rather than computing the exact integral of the function depicted in Fig. 3.9, we evaluate its value every 3 ms, over the time horizon considered, and use a Riemann sum to approximate the average end-to-end delay.

The slight inaccuracy resulting from assuming delay is constant over the high-bandwidth portion of the network is represented in Fig. 3.10. Curves show the size of the bottleneck queue, measured every millisecond or estimated using the constant delay approximation. The results presented are for a network path with two hops. The first hop is a high-bandwidth 47.5 Mb/s T3 link which is filled with a 22 Mb/s flow of exponential cross traffic. When generating cross traffic, the size of average traffic bursts is 30 kbytes. The expected delay over this link is 59 ms: 50 ms of propagation delay and 9 ms of queuing delay, on average. The second link is a low-bandwidth 400 kb/s link which only carries video traffic. Video traffic is generated by sending video frames of the *Mother & Daughter* sequence, 30 times per second, from the

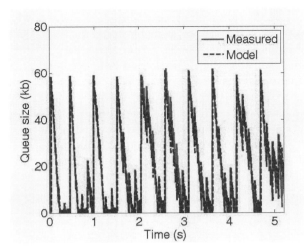

Fig. 3.10. Size of the bottleneck queue, as a function of time. Both the measured queue size and the estimated queue size are represented. The estimated queue size is obtained by considering the delay introduced over the high-bandwidth link is equal to its statistical average.

server to the client. The video is compressed at 280 kb/s, with the encoding structure shown in Fig. 3.1. Large packets are fragmented into MTU size packets at the transport layer. As illustrated, the accuracy is satisfactory.

In terms of implementation, an additional technical detail should be noted. At the end of the time horizon we consider, the bottleneck queue might not be empty. Being oblivious to the bits which remain in the bottleneck queue would favor transmission schedules where large frames are transmitted last. To alleviate this problem, the area under the function represented in Fig. 3.9 is estimated by its Riemann sum up to the time where the queue is empty (this is always possible as the schedules we consider span a limited time horizon). The average congestion, however, is derived as the ratio of this area to the length of the time horizon, $k \cdot \delta t$.

Expected Video Distortion

The performance of a given schedule in terms of video quality can be evaluated by estimating the distortion of a set of frames about to be decoded:

$$D(\pi) = \sum_f D_f(\pi) \tag{3.12}$$

In (3.12), the distortion for the set of frames is expressed as the sum of the distortion of each decoded frame of the set. This sum should be taken over all the frames which can be affected by the arrival of the scheduled packets, and should also account for any frame freeze. Therefore, when computing (3.12) at a given time, we consider the distortion of all the frames which have not yet been played out and that are available for transmission at the sender, according to the diagram shown in Fig. A.2.

The expected value of the distortion of Frame f, $D_f(\pi)$, is computed as in [79]. Namely, we consider previous frame concealment, as described in Appendix A, and assume that frames are frozen until the next decodable frame. Hence, to capture the effect of packet loss on the video quality, only a limited number of display outcomes need to be identified and associated with different distortions. Let $D(s, f)$ denote the distortion resulting from substituting Frame s to Frame f. For the schedule π the expected distortion of Frame f is expressed:

$$D_f(\pi) = \sum_{s \leq f} D(s, f) Pr\{s, f, \pi, I\} \tag{3.13}$$

Figure 3.11, shows the values of $D(s, f)$ for different sequences. In general, distortion increases as a function of $|f - s|$. However, due to oscillating motion, for 4 of the 6 sequences this is not always the case for large values of $|f - s|$. To avoid any artifact due to this effect, we replace $D(s, f)$ with the distortion resulting from showing a gray frame when $|f - s| > 2GOP\_Length$.

In (3.13), $Pr\{s, f, \pi, I\}$ represents the probability that, for transmission schedule π, Frame s is displayed instead of f. This assumes that Frame s, and all the frames it depends on, are available at the receiver at the time Frame f is due, and that no other frame, nearer to Frame f, and preceding it, is decodable.

In our particular experimental set-up, $Pr\{s, f, \pi, I\}$ incorporates the delay distribution of the high-bandwidth portion of the network and the packet loss probability after the bottleneck link. $Pr\{s, f, \pi, I\}$ may be computed, by combining the probabilities that different packets reach the client by their playout deadlines. This value also depends on additional information available at the server on the streaming session which is denoted by I. This includes the playout latency and the encoding structure of the video stream, which determines the different frame types of s and f and their place in a GOP. It also includes information the sender has collected, through feedback, about the reception status of packets transmitted in the past.

We consider, for simplicity, that the scheduler is limited to transmitting entire frames rather than the different packets composing these frames. We denote by $\epsilon_i(\pi, I)$ the probability that Frame i (i.e., Packet i) misses its decoding deadline with a given schedule π and additional information, I, available at the server. We will also use the notation ϵ_i for convenience. The derivation of these probabilities is discussed in detail in [77, 79]. Due to the time-varying bottleneck queue we consider, the derivation varies slightly in our case.

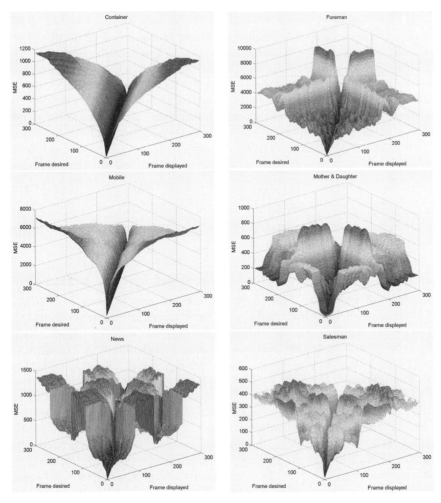

Fig. 3.11. Mean squared error distortion $D(s, f)$, for all combinations of s and f, where s is the frame displayed and f is the frame that should be displayed. Please note that for the error-concealment method employed in this work $f \geq s$, however the case $f < s$ is also shown in the graphs. The encoding rate for the different sequences is as follows. Container: 244 kb/s, Foreman: 257 kb/s, Mobile: 237 kb/s, Mother and Daughter: 282 kb/s, News: 319 kb/s, Salesman: 311 kb/s.

To illustrate this difference, we derive the probability that Frame i, transmitted at time ts_i does not reach the receiver by its decoding deadline td_i[4]. This occurs when Frame i is lost (e.g., due to a transmission error after the bottleneck link) or when it is received at time $tr_i > td_i$. In the derivation, we denote the delay over the high-bandwidth portion of the network by the random variable δ. We denote by ta_i the time at which Frame i reaches the bottleneck queue. We also assume that, when π and I are known, the scheduler can accurately compute the size of the bottleneck queue $Q(t)$, at any time t, as seen in the previous section. The probability $\epsilon_i(\pi, I)$ is derived as follows:

$$\epsilon_i(\pi, I) = P_{loss} + (1 - P_{loss}) Prob\{tr_i > td_i | \pi, I\}, \tag{3.14}$$

where, $Prob\{tr_i > td_i | \pi, I\}$

$$= Prob\{ts_i + \delta + Q(ta_i) + \frac{B_i}{C} > td_i | \pi, I\} \tag{3.15}$$

$$= Prob\{\delta + Q(ts_i + \delta) > td_i - ts_i - \frac{B_i}{C} | \pi, I\} \tag{3.16}$$

In (3.14), we express $\epsilon_i(\pi, I)$ as the combination of random losses, of rate P_{loss}, and of late losses. In (3.15), the delay of Packet i, is expressed as the sum of the delay on the high-bandwidth portion of the network, δ, of the queuing delay when the packet reaches the bottleneck queue, $Q(ta_i)$, and of the transmission time over the bottleneck, which depends on the size of Packet i, B_i and on the throughput of the link, C. The probability of late losses, as expressed in (3.16), only depends on the random variable δ and on the function Q, which can be accurately computed given the history of transmissions preceding that of Frame i, since the bottleneck link is not shared. As we assume the random delay experienced by the different packets over the high-bandwidth portion of the network to be independent and identically distributed, the different $\{\epsilon_k(\pi, I), k = 1 \cdots n\}$ are mutually independent. Please note that the probabilities of loss (and especially of late loss) of different packets are not independent in general. This property is a consequence of considering this quantity conditioned on a policy π and on the history of past transmission I, as well as a bottleneck reserved for these packets.

To simplify the computation of (3.16), we compute the late loss probability, in practice, by making the following approximation:

$$Prob\{tr_i > td_i | \pi, I\} \simeq$$

$$Prob\{\delta > td_i - ts_i - \frac{B_i}{C} - Q(ts_i + E[\delta])\} \tag{3.17}$$

In (3.17), we assume that $Q(ts_i + \delta)$ can be replaced by $Q(ts_i + E[\delta])$, where $E[\delta]$ is the expected value of δ, and includes propagation delay as well

---

[4] A frame may, of course, be transmitted more than once, as analyzed in detail in [77, 79]. This case does not provide any additional insight here.

as queuing delay over the high-bandwidth links. This assumption is justified when the variance of the delay over the high-bandwidth links is small.

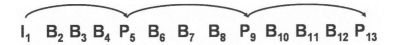

I_1 B_2 B_3 B_4 P_5 B_6 B_7 B_8 P_9 B_{10} B_{11} B_{12} P_{13}

Fig. 3.12. Encoding structure of a partial GOP containing I, P, and B frames. The numbering reflects the display order of the pictures.

The general form of the expression of $Pr\{s, f, \pi, I\}$ is intricate. However, it is not particularly difficult to compute. As an illustration, for the encoding structure shown in Fig. 3.12, we derive the probability that Frame 9 is shown instead of Frame 11. Given the schedule π and the information I, we assume the different probabilities $\{\epsilon_1, ..., \epsilon_{13}\}$ have been computed and we consider Frame 1 has been received and decoded correctly. The frames necessary to decode Frame 9 are Frame 5 and Frame 9. In addition, Frame 10 and Frame 11 should not be decodable. This implies that either Frame 13 is not received or that Frames 10 and 11 are both missing. Hence, the probability is:

$$Pr\{9, 11, \pi, I\} = (1 - \epsilon_5) \cdot (1 - \epsilon_9) \cdot (\epsilon_{13} + (1 - \epsilon_{13})\epsilon_{10}\epsilon_{11}). \qquad (3.18)$$

3.2.3 Randomized Schedule Search

In this section, we describe how to determine an efficient transmission schedule for the packets of a video stream. For a set of n packets and for k time slots, the number of possible schedules is 2^{nk}, if we allow retransmissions, since at each time slot any of the packets can potentially be sent.

In [77], an algorithm called "iterative sensitivity adjustment" is presented to overcome the problem of the exponentially growing search space, by optimizing the transmission policy for one packet at a time, while fixing the schedule for the other packets. This method is suitable when the probability of a successful transmission is independent of the schedules of other packets, as, for example, in [79, 112]. In our case, however, each packet transmission affects the arrival times of successive packets. As a result, iterative sensitivity adjustment and similar convex optimization methods would often not converge to the desired solution.

We propose, as an alternative, a randomized search algorithm to determine an efficient schedule. The algorithm is simple: a schedule for the different video packets considered is selected at random and evaluated in terms of its expected Lagrangian cost $D(\pi) + \lambda\Delta(\pi)$, according to the procedure described in Sec. 3.2.2; if the schedule outperforms all other schedules considered so far, it becomes the new reference schedule; if not, it is discarded. After a given number of iterations, packets are transmitted, at the beginning of the present time slot, according to the reference schedule. Schedules are re-optimized at each time slot, as in [77, 79, 80, 81].

We initialize the algorithm by evaluating the cost of several heuristic schedules. One of the starting points is the tail of the schedule chosen for the previous transmission opportunity. The other heuristic schedules we consider are:

- the empty schedule;
- all the schedules where only one packet is sent in the present time slot, and no other packet is sent;
- a sequential schedule, where packets which have not been transmitted yet are sent sequentially, following their frame number; to avoid congestion, successive packets are mapped to the next time slot during which the bottleneck queue is expected to become empty; if this time slot is beyond the time horizon considered, packets are not transmitted.

Interestingly, despite the fact that simple rules can often be used to determine which packets should be sent, the specific order of transmission indicated by the randomized algorithm is usually non-trivial and yields lower congestion than that of heuristic starting points.

As an illustration, we show in Fig. 3.13 the cost in terms of expected mean squared error (MSE) distortion and of average queuing delay of 300 different schedules for a set of 10 frames sent over the two-hop network path described in Sec. 3.2.2. The first hop is a high-bandwidth 47.5 Mb/s T3 link which is filled with a 22 Mb/s flow of exponential cross traffic. The second link is a low-bandwidth 400 kb/s link which only carries video traffic.

The frame numbers and their type are depicted in Fig. 3.14. The playout deadline is 600 ms. The experiment is run at the decoding time of Frame 144. The diagram shown in Fig. A.2, indicates that, at this time, and for this playout deadline, frames 145 to 164 are available at the sender. Frames 145 to 154 have already been acknowledged by the receiver, therefore they are no longer considered. None of the frames shown in Fig. 3.14 have been transmitted yet. When the experiment is run, the queue at the bottleneck is empty. We consider transmissions over the next 132 ms. This interval is divided into 4 equal time slots, at the beginning of each time slot, CoDiO may select one or several frames to transmit.

We denote by Ndu the number of packets (i.e., frames) which the scheduler considers for transmission, and by $Numts$ the number of time slots. We denote by p_t the number of packets we wish to transmit on average in a time slot (please note that this number is not restricted to be an integer), and by $rand$, a random variable, uniformly distributed between 0 and 1. CoDiO determines the $slot$ at which each data unit is transmitted as follows:

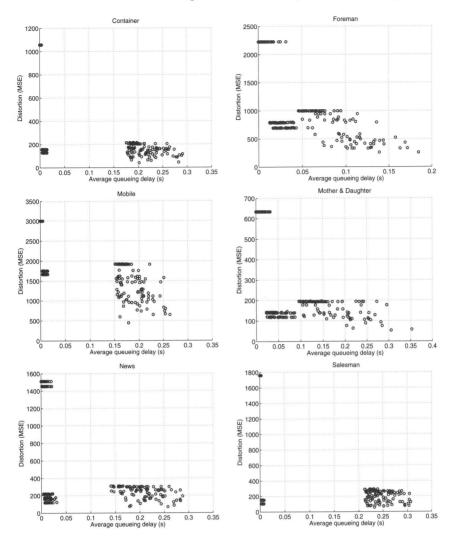

Fig. 3.13. Congestion-distortion performance of different schedules. The encoding rate for the different sequences is as follows. Container: 244 kb/s, Foreman: 257 kb/s, Mobile: 237 kb/s, Mother and Daughter: 244 kb/s, News: 319 kb/s, Salesman: 311 kb/s.

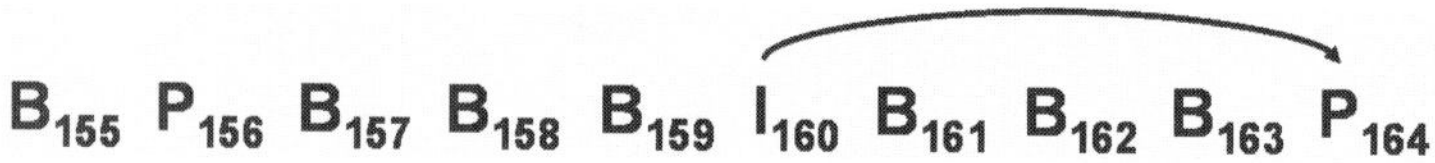

$$B_{155} \quad P_{156} \quad B_{157} \quad B_{158} \quad B_{159} \quad I_{160} \quad B_{161} \quad B_{162} \quad B_{163} \quad P_{164}$$

Fig. 3.14. Encoding structure of the frames used in the example illustrating the random schedule search.

$$slot = \lfloor \frac{rand \cdot Ndu}{p_t} \rfloor, \text{ if } rand \le p_t \frac{Numts}{Ndu}$$

$$slot = \infty, \text{ otherwise.}$$

An infinite time slot indicates that the packet is not transmitted. This simple rule allows to schedule p_t packets per time slot, and to uniformly distribute them over time slots. In the experiments presented in this chapter, we fix an average transmission rate of 1.2 frames per time slot.

As shown in Fig. 3.13, the different schedules considered vary widely both in distortion and congestion. The points in the graphs appear in clusters. The cluster in the top left corner of the graphs characterizes schedules where no I or P frames are transmitted. They lead to highest distortion as none of the frames shown in Fig. 3.14 are decodable, and to low congestion, as the B frames transmitted are relatively small. For most of the sequences, there is another cluster in the left-most portion of the graphs. This cluster represents the performance of schedules where Frame 156 is transmitted, but not the I frame. The cluster is clearly separated when the size difference between I and P frames is larger. For this particular set of frames, schedules with low distortions are arrangements in which frames 156, 160, and 164 are transmitted, as well as a varying number of the other frames shown in Fig. 3.14. As an example, we compare, in Fig. 3.15, the three schedules for which distortion is smallest, for the sequence *Mother and Daughter*. As illustrated, congestion is reduced when the transmission of the larger frames is spaced out.

To differentiate between the best performing schedules, congestion is a better suited metric than rate. For the schedules with lowest distortion, the same set of I and P frames are transmitted, leading to similar rates. However, depending on the transmission order, the resulting congestion may vary widely. This is illustrated by the performance of the schedules in terms of distortion, congestion, and rate represented in figures 3.13 and 3.16. The difference between rate and congestion is particularly pronounced for the schedules leading to lower distortion for the sequence *Mobile*. For the rate-distortion plot in Fig. 3.16, these schedules seem to form a rate-distortion curve, reflecting that the points representing several different schedules are superimposed, whereas the congestion-distortion plot in Fig. 3.13 clearly shows a difference in the congestion of these schedules.

For the examples illustrated above, choosing the scheduler with least congestion rather than the one with highest congestion, among the minimal distortion schedules, leads to a congestion reduction of between 25% and 50%,

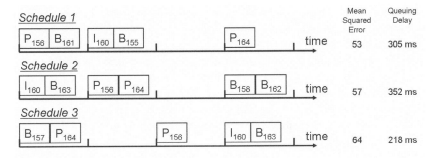

Fig. 3.15. Three schedule examples for the sequence *Mother & Daughter*, and their performance in terms of MSE and queuing delay. The size of the frames is not drawn to scale.

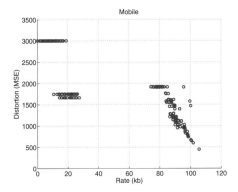

Fig. 3.16. Rate-distortion performance of different schedules for the sequence *Mobile*. The particular schedules are the same as those represented in Fig. 3.13. Rate is obtained by summing the bits transmitted within the time horizon.

depending on the sequence. This is achieved by picking a transmission order which reduces the occurrence of delay spikes at the bottleneck queue. We expect the same approximate range of performance improvement over a scheduler such as RaDiO which is oblivious to the impact it may have on queuing delay. Please note that as the average encoding rate of the sequences approaches capacity the range spanned by congestion increases, and so does the performance improvement.

3.2.4 CoDiO Light

The algorithm described in the previous section is naturally scalable, as the number of schedules considered can be reduced, at the expense of less efficient solutions. When the number of schedules considered falls below a certain threshold (around 50 for the previous examples), the quality is not satisfying. However, it is possible to reduce computational complexity by another order of magnitude. This is achieved by observing that, in the absence of cross traffic sharing the bottleneck, it is *never* advantageous to have multiple packets in the bottleneck queue at the same time. In terms of congestion, having the next packet wait in the bottleneck queue, rather than at the client creates unnecessary queuing delay. In terms of distortion, as the bottleneck queue is not shared with cross traffic, delaying the packet transmission will not alter its chances of timely arrival significantly, as long it is sent early enough. In addition, during the time it waits for the previous packet to clear the bottleneck, the client may receive new acknowledgment packets from the receiver, which may change the information I, used to compute expected distortion, and change the sequence of optimal transmissions. For the CoDiO scheduler, described in the previous sections, multiple transmissions sometimes occur back-to-back in the same time slot. This mostly depends on the parameter p_t, which controls the average number of packets sent per time slot. For time slotted schedules for which the intervals δt between different transmission opportunities is long enough to transmit more than one frame (this is typically the case for B frames), when several packets are yet to be transmitted, CoDiO will schedule several packets in the same time slot, rather than leaving the bottleneck queue empty for part of the time slot, as this may reduce expected distortion.

The low-complexity scheduler, *CoDiO light*, determines iteratively the best next packet to send in terms of the Lagrangian cost $D+\lambda\Delta$. This is carried out by comparing all the schedules where only one packet is sent in the present time slot, and no other packet is sent. Note that these schedules are also considered by CoDiO as heuristic starting points. The best of these schedules is determined by evaluating their cost, based on the methodology described in Sec. 3.2.2. A packet is sent when one of these schedules outperforms the empty schedule.

The best-next-packet selection is repeated after waiting for the time needed for the last packet to drain from the bottleneck queue. For Packet i, of size B_i, this time is simply B_i/C, where C is the capacity of the bottleneck. Please note, that due to propagation delay, a packet will actually be sent while the previous packet is still in the bottleneck queue. However, the new packet is expected to *arrive* at the bottleneck when the queue becomes empty. As an additional technical detail, when the empty schedule performs best, CoDiO light is run again after 5 ms. The computational load of CoDiO light is typically only 1/100th of that required for CoDiO.

The adaptive spacing of successive transmissions is essential for the performance of CoDiO light. We also considered regular time slots, spaced every 33 ms, similar to CoDiO. Experimental results were not satisfying. The adaptive spacing, however, leads to excellent performance, as will be shown in Sec. 3.2.5.

3.2.5 Experimental Results

Experimental Setup

The different schedulers are evaluated by simulating the transmission of video streams in the network simulator ns-2. Results presented are for a low-latency streaming scenario where a sender transmits video frames to the receiver which sends ACKs back for each frame it has received. We consider a network path with two hops, as described in Sec. 3.2.2. The first hop is a lossless high-bandwidth duplex 47.5 Mb/s T3 link which is filled with a 22 Mb/s flow of exponential cross traffic. When generating cross traffic, the size of average traffic bursts is 30 kbytes. The expected delay over this link is 59 ms: 50 ms of propagation delay and 9 ms of queuing delay, on average. The second link is a lossy low-bandwidth duplex 400 kb/s link which only carries video traffic. We consider a fixed packet loss rate of 2% over this link. The propagation delay over the link is 2 ms. We assume that the scheduler has perfect knowledge of the delay distribution over the high-bandwidth links, of the bottleneck capacity, and of the packet loss rate.

We let CoDiO and CoDiO light consider transmissions of entire frames only, and large video packets are fragmented into MTU size packets at the transport layer. ACKs are sent when all the packets of a frame have been received. When a frame has been transmitted, it is no longer considered for transmission until the probability that it has been lost reaches 95%. This occurs, in the absence of an ACK, soon after the expected reception time of the ACK. For CoDiO scheduling, we consider schedules which cover the next 132 ms. This interval is divided into 4 equal time slots, at the beginning of each time slot, CoDiO may select one or several frames to transmit. Transmission for the present time slot are determined by choosing the best out of 100 schedules. Schedules are re-optimized at each time slot. The maximum average number of frames sent per time slot is set to $p_t = 1.2$, as in the experiments shown in Sec. 3.2.3[5]. If a schedule indicates more than one transmission in a time slot, these occur back-to-back, following the sequence number of the packets. For CoDiO light, the spacing between successive transmissions depends on the size of the previous frame sent, as described in Sec. 3.2.4.

Results are presented for six video sequences compressed using the coding structure depicted in Fig. 3.1. The encoding rate for the different sequences is as follows. The encoding rate for the different sequences is as follows, Container: 327 kb/s, Foreman: 290 kb/s, Mobile: 342 kb/s, Mother & Daughter: 319 kb/s, News: 358 kb/s, Salesman: 364 kb/s. Sequences are looped 40 times when collecting experimental results. When a packet arrives at the receiver after its playout deadline, the frame it belongs to is discarded as if it were lost. In this case, the frame is concealed using previous frame concealment and

---

[5] Please note that this only influences the way CoDiO selects schedules and does not indicate that 20% of the frames are retransmitted, as there is no unnecessary transmission or retransmission.

frozen until the next decodable frame, as described in detail in Appendix A. The results collected are the sender's transmission rate, the decoded video quality, measured in PSNR and computed as explained in Appendix A, and the congestion (i.e., the average end-to-end delay). The latter is computed by sending 1 byte probe messages every 20 ms from the sender to the receiver[6]. The average delay of these messages during the experiment indicates the level of congestion.

Determining an Optimal λ

Values for the parameter λ are determined experimentally for each of the sequences and are indicated in Tab. 3.1. This is done by running the CoDiO scheduler for different values of λ with a playout deadline of 450 ms, and choosing the one which maximizes the decoded video quality. In practice, the limiting factor in setting λ is to pick a small enough value so that all the I frames of a sequence get transmitted. Namely, the Lagrangian cost $D + \lambda\Delta$ when an I frame is transmitted should be smaller than the average distortion resulting from concealing this I frame. As the level of activity of the sequences varies vastly from sequence to sequence and leads to large differences in the efficiency of error-concealment, and as the sizes of I frames also vary significantly, this leads to λ values which span several orders of magnitude, depending on the sequence. For these values of λ, the weight given to distortion is high, compared to congestion, when computing the Lagrangian cost $D + \lambda\Delta$. Interestingly, these settings lead to far lower distortion than $\lambda = 0$. This seems to contradict the notion that CoDiO performs a trade-off between distortion D and congestion Δ. However, CoDiO considers the Lagrangian cost function $D + \lambda\Delta$ with a limited time horizon and expected distortion is computed for the set of frames available at the sender for transmission. Therefore, if $\lambda = 0$, the best decision is to send all frames at once, regardless of the congestion this causes. If at the next transmission time, an I frame enters the set of frames considered by the scheduler for transmission, the time it will have to reach the receiver might be smaller than the queuing delay created by the previous transmissions. Limiting the congestion by setting λ to the values indicated in Tab. 3.1 mitigates this problem.

Automatic Repeat reQuest (ARQ) Scheduler

In the experiments presented in the next section, we compare the performance of CoDiO and CoDiO light to an ARQ scheduler which sends video frames, as soon as they are made available to the sender, according to the process depicted in Fig. A.2, and keeps them in its buffer as long as they are not past due. When the scheduler receives an ACK for Video Frame n, it is removed

---

[6] While it is not possible to send 1 byte packets on a real network, this *is* possible in the network simulator.

Table 3.1. Values of λ for CoDiO and CoDiO light, for different sequences, expressed in s^{-1}.

Sequence	λ
Container	7
Foreman	200
Mobile	15
Mother & Daughter	1
News	5
Salesman	1

from the buffer. If this ACK is received out of order, the scheduler retransmits all the frames which were transmitted before Frame n and that have remained in its buffer, as these are packets that should have been acknowledged before Frame n.

CoDiO vs. RaDiO

We compare the performance of CoDiO vs. RaDiO in terms of distortion, rate and congestion in Fig. 3.17, 3.18 and 3.19. For RaDiO, we follow exactly the procedure used for CoDiO except that we evaluate different schedules in terms of their expected Lagrangian cost $D(\pi) + \lambda R(\pi)$. Values for the parameter λ are determined experimentally for each of the 6 sequences, in the same way as they were for CoDiO. They are indicated in Tab. 3.2. The value of R is obtained by computing the average transmitted rate over the time horizon considered. All the other parameters and algorithms remain the same (time horizon, schedule length, randomized search to determine an efficient schedule, etc.). In particular, we use the same time-varying delay distribution to estimate the probability that packets are received by a given deadline. Therefore, the impact of the sender on the channel is included through the expected distortion estimation carried out when running RaDiO.

Table 3.2. Values of λ for RaDiO, for different sequences, expressed in s/Mb.

Sequence	λ
Container	10
Foreman	1250
Mobile	10
Mother & Daughter	1
News	1
Salesman	1

The results in terms of rate and distortion for the two schedulers are almost identical as illustrated in Fig. 3.17 and 3.18. However, the curves in Fig. 3.19 show the congestion created by CoDiO is lower than that created by RaDiO. Depending on the sequence, congestion is reduced by 13% to 28%. As congestion (defined as the average end-to-end delay) includes 52 ms of delay propagation, the queuing delay is actually reduced by 20% to 40%.

For the values of λ chosen for RaDiO, the weight given to distortion is high, compared to rate, when computing the Lagrangian cost $D + \lambda R$. Therefore, both RaDiO and CoDiO are expected to choose schedules which minimize distortion. In the experiments we present, when the playout deadline is above 0.7 s, both RaDiO and CoDiO achieve almost optimal performance: they transmit all the frames to the receiver and retransmit the ones that are lost due to random losses. In this case, their transmission rate is slightly above the rate at which the sequence is encoded, due to retransmissions. When the playout deadline is between 0.3 s and 0.7 s, the performance of both schedulers slightly drops compared to the maximum performance. This drop is due to I frame retransmissions. Indeed, when an I frame is dropped, the time between which it is made available to the sender and the time at which it will reach the receiver after being retransmitted is mostly between 0.3 s and 0.7 s, as illustrated in Tab. 3.3. Hence, when an I frame is lost, both RaDiO and CoDiO will not be able to retransmit it, after the loss is detected, the rest of the GOP will be dropped which explains the corresponding slight rate drop. In this case, it is also expected that the rate and distortion of both CoDiO and RaDiO be the same. The sharp drop-off corresponds to the transmission time of the largest I frame in the sequence. Beyond this critical point, the performance of any scheduler would decrease sharply.

Table 3.3. Size of the smallest and largest I frame (in bits), and time (in seconds) needed to transmit the smallest I frame (Time 1) and the largest I frame (Time 2), assuming they are lost once. We denote the size of an I frame by B, the channel capacity by C and the propagation delay by t_p. Time 1 (or Time 2) is then $2(\frac{B}{C} + t_p) + t_p$, illustrating that in addition to transmitting the I frame twice, the scheduler also waits enough time to notice the absence of an ACK.

Sequence	Smallest I frame	Time 1	Largest I frame	Time 2
Container	96400 bit	0.69 s	100000 bit	0.71 s
Foreman	31600 bit	0.37 s	85900 bit	0.64 s
Mobile	91600 bit	0.67 s	103500 bit	0.74 s
Mother & Daughter	60400 bit	0.51 s	67300 bit	0.55 s
News	73100 bit	0.58 s	78400 bit	0.60 s
Salesman	96500 bit	0.69 s	99300 bit	0.70 s

Despite the similar rate-distortion performance we have just analyzed, the congestion created by CoDiO is lower than that of RaDiO. This difference is due to the fact that RaDiO is oblivious to the burstiness of the bitstream sent over the bottleneck link, as long as queuing does not create excessive delays causing some packets to arrive late. This is a consequence of the rate metric which does not adequately capture the impact of the order in which packets are transmitted over the network. Indeed, RaDiO will not differentiate between several schedules achieving equal rate-distortion performance, whereas CoDiO picks the one with least congestion. This is illustrated by the difference between Fig. 3.13 and Fig. 3.16 which was highlighted in Sec. 3.2.3.

This effect is further analyzed in Fig. 3.20, which shows the variation of end-to-end delay as a function of time. The trace corresponds to the 10 first seconds of the experiment analyzed in Fig. 3.17, Fig. 3.18, and Fig. 3.19 for a playout of 550 ms. Please note that end-to-end delay includes 52 ms of propagation delay. Also, probe packets which serve to measure end-to-end delay, are only sent after the first second which explains why there are no results for the first second. The curves shown in the figure allow to track the size of the bottleneck queue. Delay spikes every 0.5 s are due to the presence of I frames at the beginning of each GOP. In some cases, I frame retransmissions can be seen, as, for example, for the sequence *Mother & Daughter* at Time 1.8 s for CoDiO, and at time 7.5 s for RaDiO. The average rate for this particular period of time is also reported in the caption of Fig. 3.20, to ensure that the differences in performance between the two schedulers is not only caused by differences in terms of rate. The figure illustrates that CoDiO does not let packets accumulate in the bottleneck queue. This is particularly significant for *Foreman*, *News*, and *Mother & Daughter*, where the transmitted rate actually exceeds that of RaDiO, even though congestion is lower. For *Mobile* and *Container*, P frames and B frames are very small compared to I frames, and no real packet accumulation can be observed (except when an I frame is retransmitted). This is corroborated by the instantaneous rate variations shown in Appendix A, which illustrate that traffic patterns are very regular for these two sequences. This explains why smaller performance differences are observed for these sequences in Fig. 3.19.

CoDiO, CoDiO Light, and ARQ

Figures 3.21, 3.22 and 3.23, illustrate the performance, in terms of PSNR, rate and congestion of CoDiO and CoDiO light compared to the ARQ scheduler. Results are shown for different playout deadlines. The value of λ for CoDiO and CoDiO light is indicated in Tab. 3.1. As shown in Fig. 3.21, CoDiO and CoDiO light clearly outperform the ARQ scheduler. Depending on the sequences and on the playout deadline, the gap between the schedulers ranges from 1 dB to 4 dB in terms of video quality, and the congestion reduction ranges from 25% up to 75%.

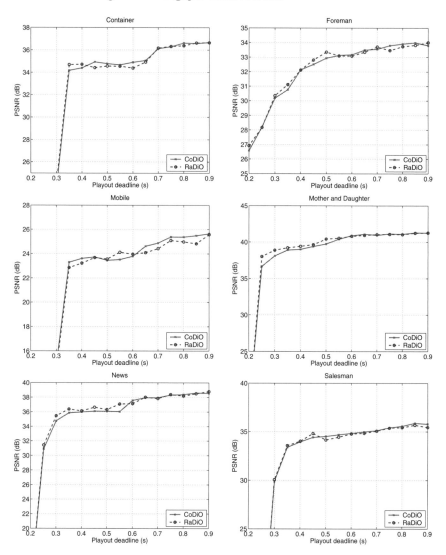

Fig. 3.17. Performance of CoDiO in terms of video quality compared to RaDiO for different playout deadlines.

The performance gap between CoDiO (or CoDiO light) and ARQ is caused by the larger congestion created by the ARQ scheduler on the bottleneck link. Sometimes, the transmitted rate of ARQ even exceeds capacity, which leads to very bad performance. This is due to the fact that ARQ always transmits all the packets of the video stream, and keeps retransmitting lost packets as long as they are not past due (i.e., as long as their playout deadline has not gone by). As ARQ does not use a model for the delay between the sender and

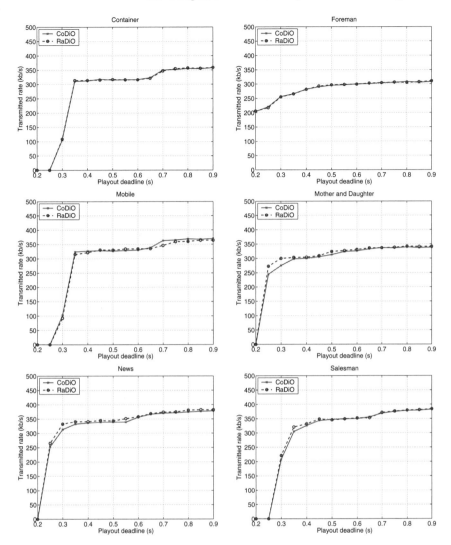

Fig. 3.18. Performance of CoDiO in terms of rate compared to RaDiO for different playout deadlines.

the receiver, some of these retransmissions are wasted. These unnecessary transmissions increase congestion which in turn increases the occurrence of late losses. CoDiO or CoDiO light, on the other hand, do not send packets which will not meet their playout deadline. For shorter playout deadlines (i.e., less than 0.7 s), this results in lower transmission rates, lower congestion, and allows packets which *do* have time to meet their playout deadline and which *will* improve the video quality to reach the receiver. The performance gap is larger when the transmitted rate approaches capacity, due to the large growth

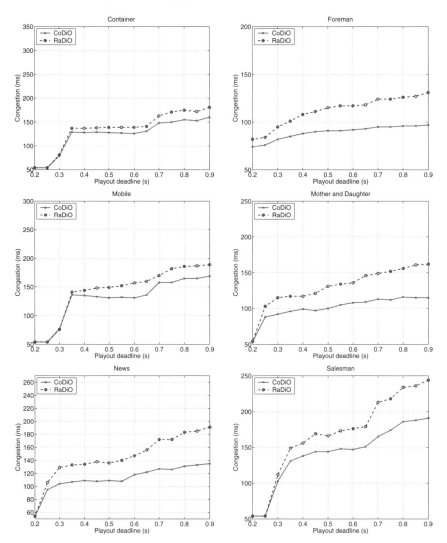

Fig. 3.19. Performance of CoDiO in terms of congestion compared to RaDiO for different playout deadlines. Congestion is defined as the average end-to-end delay and includes 52 ms of propagation delay.

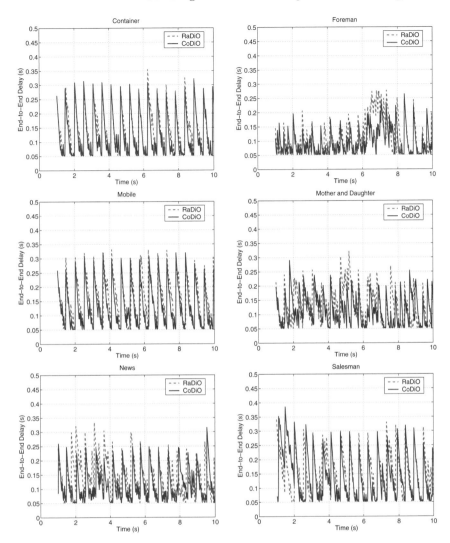

Fig. 3.20. End-to-end delay for CoDiO and RaDiO schedulers. The average rates for this period for CoDiO and RaDiO are as follows. For CoDiO, Container: 327 kb/s, Foreman: 315 kb/s, Mobile: 347 kb/s, Mother & Daughter: 343 kb/s, News: 366 kb/s, Salesman: 349 kb/s. For RaDiO, Container: 324 kb/s, Foreman: 306 kb/s, Mobile: 348 kb/s, Mother & Daughter: 333 kb/s, News: 374 kb/s, Salesman: 364 kb/s.

of the bottleneck queue caused by ARQ. The performance gap also increases, when the playout deadline decreases, as in this case, the absence of congestion is crucial.

The figures also allow to compare the performance of CoDiO and CoDiO light. With the exception of congestion, which is lower for CoDiO light, there is not much difference between the results obtained with the two schedulers. The much lower computational complexity of CoDiO light allows us to determine new schedules at much more frequent intervals than we do with CoDiO (every 5 ms, compared to every 33 ms). As a consequence, the congestion for CoDiO light scheduler is lower than for CoDiO, as it always waits for the queue to drain before the next transmission. CoDiO, on the other hand, sometimes sends several packets in the same time slot, as depicted, for example, in Fig. 3.15, this causes higher congestion. In addition, the shorter time slots of CoDiO light make for a scheme which is more reactive to feedback information and which minimizes the time the bottleneck link is left idle. This improves the overall performance and, therefore, CoDiO light sometimes outperforms CoDiO, even though it chooses from a smaller subset of transmission schedules. Examining the set of packets transmitted by CoDiO and CoDiO light reveals that, despite the difference in the order in which packets are transmitted, there is no significant difference between the packets selected by the schedulers, except those due to retransmission of lost packets.

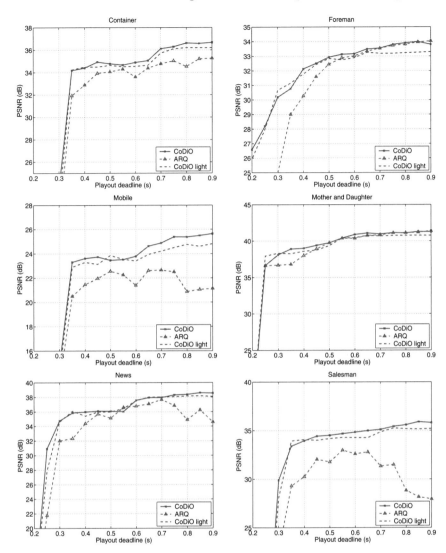

Fig. 3.21. Performance of CoDiO and CoDiO light in terms of video quality compared to an ARQ scheduler for different playout deadlines.

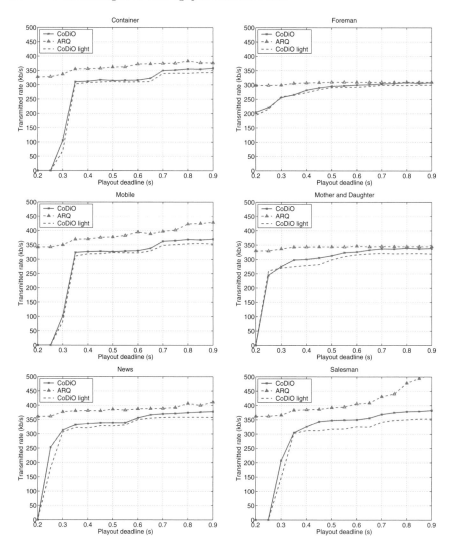

Fig. 3.22. Performance of CoDiO and CoDiO light in terms of rate compared to an ARQ scheduler for different playout deadlines.

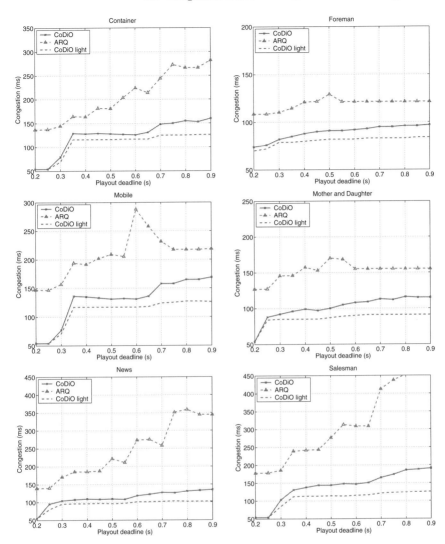

Fig. 3.23. Performance of CoDiO and CoDiO light in terms of congestion compared to an ARQ scheduler for different playout deadlines.

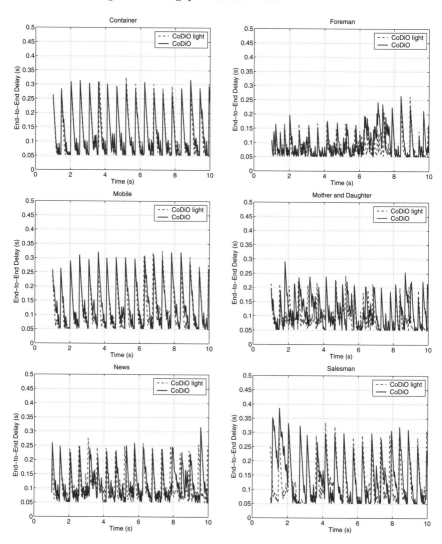

Fig. 3.24. End-to-end delay for CoDiO and CoDiO light.

3.3 Chapter Summary

In this chapter we analyze the influence of the encoding rate of a sequence on the end-to-end performance of a low-latency video streaming system. The model we present incorporates contributions from both encoder distortion and packet loss due to network congestion. In this context, the optimal rate for video streaming allows the compressed video stream to achieve a high video quality without creating significant congestion on the network. Experimental results for different video sequences over a simulated network are presented for a typical server-client scenario. The model captures the influence of different parameters such as the playout deadline and the throughput of the path and can be used to predict the end-to-end rate-distortion performance.

For very low-latency streaming, we present a scheduling algorithm which, for a given level of congestion, maximizes the expected video quality. The scheduler is based on the popular rate-distortion optimization framework introduced by [77] but uses a new metric and a novel randomized search algorithm to determine efficient packet transmission schedules. We also describe a low-complexity version of the scheduler which achieves similar performance and is light enough to run in real-time. For rates approaching capacity, CoDiO largely outperforms a conventional ARQ scheduler in terms of congestion, distortion and rate. By considering congestion as a better-suited metric to evaluate the performance of different schedules, CoDiO achieves the same rate-distortion results as the state-of-the-art scheduler RaDiO, but reduces the queuing delay created on the bottleneck link by up to 40%.

Our results lead to the following conclusions:

- As congestion is an increasing function of rate, rate-distortion and congestion-distortion schedulers have similar rate-distortion performance.
- For the same reason, a rate constraint also indirectly limits congestion.
- One need not trade off rate and congestion. Congestion can be lowered without increasing rate: this is achieved by "just-in-time" delivery, where packets are held at the server, rather than on the bottleneck queues of the network.

A congestion constraint exhibits additional advantages. As it depends on throughput, it is naturally adaptive to network conditions. Moreover, shaping traffic to reduce self-congestion not only benefits a low-latency streaming session as highlighted in this chapter, but also results in less congestion for other users of the network. Therefore, we conclude that congestion is a better metric than rate for video streaming.

4

Peer-to-Peer Control Protocol

Peer-to-peer (P2P) streaming systems take advantage of the forwarding capacity of their users to distribute media, in real-time, to large audiences. As the network fabric is unreliable, since any of the peers may choose to disconnect from the system at any time, the performance of such systems depends on a number of factors including the efficiency and robustness of the control protocol responsible for maintaining connections among the users. The control protocol is responsible for establishing different transmission trees which connect the different peers participating in the video multicast. These trees are rooted at the source and the branches of each tree link a peer to its descendants. Complementary portions of the video stream are distributed over the different trees and peers need to join *each* of the multiple trees to decode and playout the entire video successfully. As video traffic is relayed by the peers along the different branches of the multicast trees, the video source need only directly serve a small subset of peers. This approach is self-scaling, in theory, as long as the video traffic rate does not exceed the average throughput contributed by the peers.

In this chapter, we describe in detail the Stanford Peer-to-Peer Multicast protocol (SPPM), designed primarily by Jeonghun Noh. The SPPM protocol protocol organizes peer nodes in an overlay that consists of a set of complementary multicast trees. It enables a source to distribute a video stream to a population of peers via P2P multicast and has been specifically targeted at low startup latency.

Our goal is to provide, through a description of this example, an overview of the different steps necessary to setup connections between different peers of a P2P live streaming network. A general understanding of the protocol is important to grasp the adaptive video streaming techniques presented in Chapter 5 which enhance the performance of the system and provide error resilience. SPPM has recently been deployed over PlanetLab [208], and the performance analysis presented in [209] confirms the experimental evaluation described in this chapter.

In the next section, we explain, in detail, how connections are built and maintained in a distributed fashion by the protocol to enable different peers to cooperate in relaying video traffic. In Sec. 4.2, we describe our experimental setup and present a performance analysis of the control protocol. We study, in particular, its latency and overhead. Finally we provide insights on the limits of the system by testing its scalability and determining the rate it can support.

4.1 Protocol Description

The control protocol is run by each peer wishing to participate in the multicast session. The design of the protocol distinguishes between two hierarchical levels. The first level corresponds to the peer and how it transitions between different states (this level is denoted by the term "peer" in the following), the second corresponds to the connections the peer maintains to each of the multicast trees it will join to receive the full video stream, (this level is denoted by the term "tree connection"). Managing the state transitions of the trees is the most important part of the protocol. The legend for the different diagrams we will use to describe protocol operations is shown in Fig. 4.1.

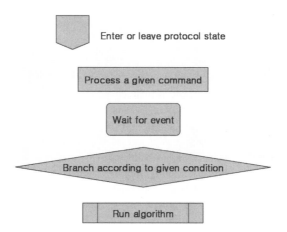

Fig. 4.1. Legend for protocol state diagrams.

4.1.1 Different Peer States

Each peer can be in one of four states: OFFLINE, JOIN, PROBE and ONLINE. The peer level is responsible for a limited number of tasks which have to do with initialization and basic connection maintenance. The OFFLINE state corresponds to an inactive peer, the peer can transition to this state from any other state; in this case, any connection to other peers of the network is interrupted and the peer is unresponsive. When a peer wants to join the multicast, it enters the JOIN state.

JOIN State

The operations in the JOIN state, at the peer level, are described in Fig. 4.2. In this initial phase, the peer exchanges a message with the source of the multicast to obtain a list of connected peers which it will contact, subsequently, to join the session. In addition to transmitting this list, the source informs the peer of the number of multicast trees over which the video stream is transmitted, as well as the rate necessary to support the stream. As soon as the reply from the source is received, the peer creates the corresponding number of trees and transitions to the state PROBE. The state of the trees is set to OFFLINE (this state, at the tree level, will be discussed in the following). In our experiments, we assume the address of the source is known to all the peers.

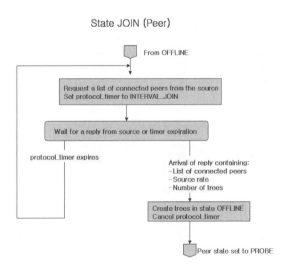

Fig. 4.2. Protocol operations for the peer in JOIN state.

PROBE State

As illustrated in Fig. 4.3, when the peer transitions to the PROBE state, probing messages are sent to all the members of the list of connected peers which was transmitted by the source. In their replies, peers indicate their available amount of throughput as well as their height in the different multicast trees (i.e. the number of hops separating them from the source).

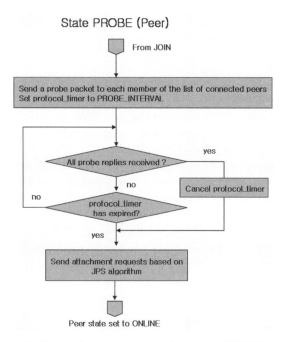

Fig. 4.3. Protocol operations for the peer in PROBE state.

Parents which have enough throughput to support an additional peer connection are selected based on the Joint Parent Selection (JPS) algorithm, detailed in the diagram in Fig. 4.4. Each tree is considered, iteratively and, if possible, different parents are chosen for the different trees to make use of diversity. Among the parent candidates, the peer will choose the one which is closest to the source in the multicast tree considered. This limits the depth of the trees being constructed. After the selection of candidates for each tree, attachment requests are sent out and the state of the trees is set to ATTACH. The state of trees for which there is no available parent is set to JOIN. Both these states will be described in the following. In most cases, all the trees have an identical number of potential parent candidates. However, this might not be the case when the source itself is a potential candidate, as we require the source to accept the same number of children for each tree, so as to prevent any unevenness. In this particular case, considering peers with the smallest number of candidate parents, first, results in a better use of the available throughput.

Several other criteria could also be considered in this process. For example, the amount of available throughput, the round-trip time (RTT) or geographical proximity. Similarly to the results reported in [210], we observed in [199] that building minimum-depth trees, compared to minimizing the RTT, lead to more stable structures as they increase the average uninterrupted connection time of peers to the multicast trees.

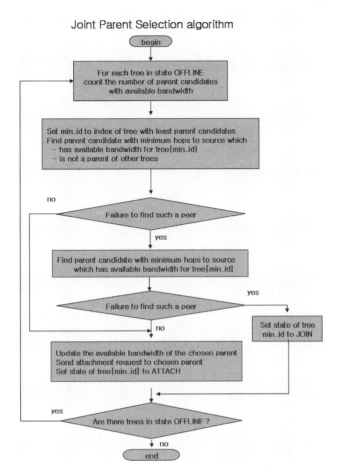

Fig. 4.4. Joint Parent Selection algorithm.

After this initial connection establishment, managed jointly for all the trees at the peer level, the different trees operate independently except in the REJOIN state illustrated in Fig. 4.11 and in the Single Parent Selection algorithm shown in Fig. 4.10 and discussed below. After the JPS algorithm is run, the peer enters and remains in the ONLINE state until is is switched off.

ONLINE State

The connection of the trees to their different parents is monitored at regular intervals by the peer, as illustrated in Fig. 4.5, by running the algorithm Check Parent shown in Fig. 4.6.

Disconnections are detected by monitoring the arrival of video traffic and probe responses. To maintain an efficient tree structure, a peer will also disconnect from a parent which responds to probing but does not forward video

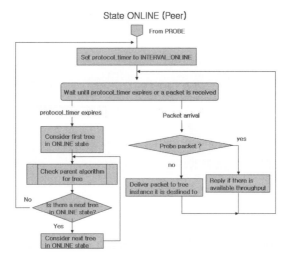

Fig. 4.5. Protocol operations for the peer in PROBE state.

traffic. We observed that it is worthwhile to minimize false detections of disconnections at the expense of longer traffic interruptions, since losses may be mitigated by retransmissions. If the connection of one of the trees has failed, its state is set to REJOIN. In this case, the video streaming protocol will be informed of the state of the trees to avoid sending packet retransmission requests to disconnected parents.

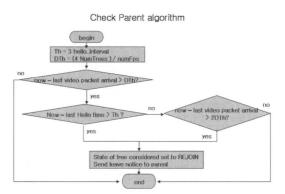

Fig. 4.6. Check parent algorithm. The number of frames per second sent by the video streaming protocol is denoted by numFps. The number of multicast trees maintained by the protocol is denoted by numTrees.

All the packets received by the peer are processed at the tree level except probe messages. In the ONLINE state, if it has more available throughput than that required to maintain an additional child on one of the trees, the peer will reply to these messages by indicating its available amount of throughput and its height in the different multicast trees.

4.1.2 Different Tree Connection States

A tree connection can be in one of 6 states: OFFLINE, JOIN, PROBE, AT-TACH, ONLINE and REJOIN. The tree connection only remains in the OF-FLINE state between the time it is created and the time the JPS algorithm is run.

JOIN State

A tree connection state is set to JOIN when the JPS algorithm fails to determine a suitable parent candidate for the tree or when attempts to establish a connection to a parent fail in the ATTACH or the REJOIN state.

The set of operations taken to transition from the JOIN state to the PROBE state are almost identical as the ones outlined at the peer level and are illustrated in Fig. 4.7. The only difference is due to the fact that trees connections do not have to be created following the reception of the reply of the source.

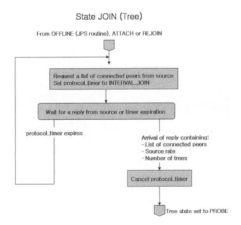

Fig. 4.7. Protocol operations in state JOIN.

PROBE State

In the PROBE state, probe messages are transmitted to the different members of the list of connected peers. As shown in Fig. 4.8, when reply messages are received, the state of the tree connection is set to ATTACH. It is in this state that a suitable parent will be determined.

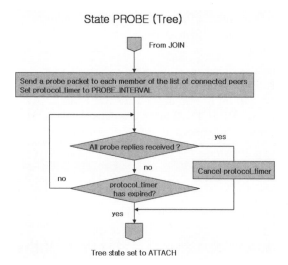

Fig. 4.8. Protocol operations in state PROBE.

ATTACH State

When the tree connection is in the state ATTACH, different candidate parents are queried for attachment, iteratively, until a successful connection is established. Candidate parents are either determined by the JPS algorithm or by the Single Parent Selection (SPS) algorithm depending on what was the state of the tree connection preceding the transition to the ATTACH state, as shown in Fig. 4.9. As attachment requests are only sent to parents which have previously indicated they have available throughput, the first attempt is usually successful. The positive acknowledgment of the attachment sent by the parent also contains additional information which is retrieved by the peer and continuously updated in the ONLINE state. The information about the parent, which is maintained by the peer for each tree connection, includes the amount of available throughput of the parent, its level in the tree, an estimate of the round-trip time between the child and the parent, the list of upstream hosts separating the peer and the source in this tree, and the time the last hello message reply was received from the parent.

Before entering the ONLINE state, the peer sets the protocol timer which will indicate when a hello message should be send to the parent. It also sends a notice to the source of the multicast indicating it has successfully established a connection to the tree and can serve as a parent candidate for other peers looking to join the session.

The SPS algorithm is illustrated in Fig. 4.10. It is run in the ATTACH state when a peer needs to select a suitable parent candidate in one of the trees. Similarly to the JPS algorithm, the SPS algorithm attempts to minimize the

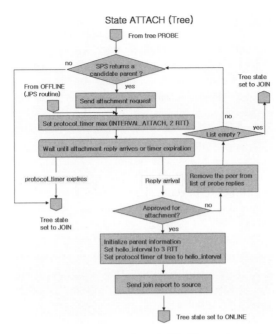

Fig. 4.9. Protocol operations in state ATTACH. The estimated round-trip time to a parent is denoted by RTT.

tree height while maximizing diversity by selecting parents as close as possible to the source which are not parents of the peer in the other trees.

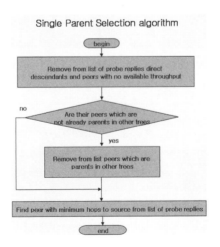

Fig. 4.10. Single Parent Selection algorithm.

REJOIN State

Ungraceful disconnections occur when a peer leaves the multicast without notice. This disrupts the connection of its descendants. After leaving the multicast, the peer stops forwarding video packets and is unresponsive. When a peer detects it has lost its connection to one of the trees through the Check Parent algorithm described above, it will enter the REJOIN state.

As illustrated in Fig. 4.11, the peer will try to rebuild a connection by choosing one of the remaining parents. If this fast recovery mechanism succeeds, the tree connection state will be set to ONLINE. If it fails, the tree connection state will be set to JOIN and the source will be contacted to obtain a new list of candidate parents. Please note that while hosts reconnect, retransmission requests are issued over the other multicast trees to recover missing video packets.

In the REJOIN state, the peer will also process control packets it may receive on this tree. Hello messages from its children will be answered and children which may decide to disconnect from the peer will be deleted from the children list when a leave notice message is received. Attachment requests will be ignored.

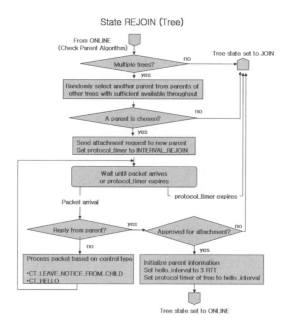

Fig. 4.11. Protocol operations in state REJOIN.

State ONLINE (Tree)

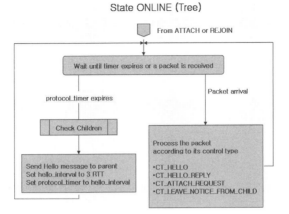

Fig. 4.12. Protocol operations in state ONLINE.

ONLINE State

Except when connections are being (re)established, tree connections remain in the ONLINE state. At the tree connection level, the peer will inform its parents of its presence by transmitting periodic "hello" messages, as shown in Fig. 4.12. Reception of a hello message generates an immediate response intended to confirm the parent's presence. In addition to verifying the connection, these messages are also used to exchange information between two neighboring peers.

The child includes in the messages the size of the subtree below it. This number is aggregated from the bottom of the tree to the top, it is used by the prioritized video streaming algorithm described in Chapter 5. Based on the exchange of hello messages, the child estimates the round-trip time to its parent, using a moving average. We denote by $RTT_{stored_{old}}$ the previous estimated round-trip time, by RTT_{new} the latest round-trip time measurement and by RTT_{stored} the new estimated round-trip time which is estimated as follows:

$$RTT_{stored} = 0.7 RTT_{stored_{old}} + 0.3 RTT_{new}.$$

When replying to a hello message, parents transmit their available throughput and the list of peers separating them from the source. This ensures a host does not reconnect to one of its descendants when it is disconnected from a multicast tree.

When an attachment request is received and there is enough available throughput, the requesting peer will become a child on the corresponding multicast tree. Information such as its address, its number of descendants and the last time a hello message has been received is initialized. A reply message is sent back to the peer indicating whether or not the attachment has been successful. In addition, the available throughput of the peer will be decreased by the source rate divided by the number of multicast trees.

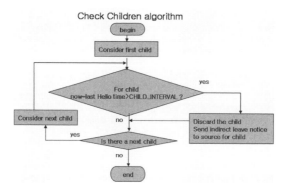

Fig. 4.13. Check children algorithm.

The peer will also periodically check the presence of its children by running the Check Children algorithm shown in Fig. 4.13. Detecting the disconnection of a child is not so critical to the overall performance as it only results in a temporary waste of the parent's network resources. Since the penalty of a false child leave detection is high, a longer time interval is used (on the order of a few seconds). When a child leave is detected, parents will remove it from their forwarding table and inform the source to purge it from the list of connected peers, if it has logged off. This is carried out by sending the source an explicit leave notification message.

4.1.3 Multicast Source

Although it plays a central role in the multicast, the source shares most of the functionalities of the peers. It is continuously in the ONLINE state, both at the peer and at the tree connection level, and processes probe messages, attachment requests, leave notices and hello messages in the same way as the other members of the session.

In addition, the multicast source is responsible for maintaining and transmitting the list of peers connected to the session. New peers are added to the list when they inform the source they have successfully established a connection to one of the trees. They are deleted when a peer detects a child has left and notifies the source, as illustrated in Fig. 4.13.

To control the overhead created by the peers in the probing state, when probing messages are sent out to discover parent candidates, the source adjusts the size of the list sent to joining peers according to the current group size and the number of multicast trees. At the beginning of the session, the group size is small and the list size corresponds to the group size. When the group size reaches a certain point, the list size increases logarithmically. For multiple trees, the source sends a larger list to allow a joining peer to better exploit path diversity. The exact size of the list, Ls, as a function of the number of connected members n and the number of trees $numTrees$ is:

$$Ls = n, \text{ if } n < 3numTrees$$
$$= \lfloor 5\ln(n - (5numTrees - 3)) + 3numTrees - 5\ln(5) + 0.5 \rfloor, \text{ otherwise.}$$
$$(4.1)$$

Figure 4.14 illustrates the size of the list sent to the peers as a function of the number of members of the session and of the number of trees.

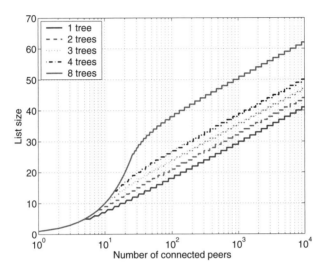

Fig. 4.14. Size of the list of connected peers transmitted by the source as a function of the number of members of the multicast session. The curves are shown on a semi-logarithmic scale for different numbers of trees.

4.1.4 Protocol Settings

Protocol Timers

Table 4.1, indicates the different time intervals which are used by the protocol and which were indicated in the protocol state diagrams described in the previous sections. The interval used to detect that the source or another peer has ignored a message in the JOIN, PROBE and ATTACH states is 0.5 s. When a peer is rejoining, this interval may be larger, depending on the round-trip time estimate. The connection state of the parents is checked 30 times per second. Finally, a child is considered to have left the multicast when it does not send hello messages for more than 2.0 seconds.

Table 4.1. Timer and time threshold settings.

INTERVAL_JOIN	0.5 s
PROBE_INTERVAL	0.5 s
INTERVAL_ATTACH	0.5 s
INTERVAL_REJOIN	max(0.5 s, 3RTT+0.3 s)
INTERVAL_ONLINE	0.033 s
CHILD_INTERVAL	2.0 s

Protocol Packet Sizes

Table 4.2 indicates the size of the different control packets used to simulate the P2P protocol in NS-2.

As stated above, we assume that the protocol runs over the UDP/IP protocol stack. The size of these headers is 8 and 20 bytes, respectively. All the messages need to include a packet type field to be identified by the receivers (this can be signalled in less than 4 bits). The LIST_REQUEST, JOIN_REPORT and PROBE messages do not require any other information, as the protocol can take advantage of the information included in the IP and UDP header. The ATTACH_REQUEST and LEAVE_NOTICE messages should indicate, in addition, the tree they are destined to (4 bits). For all these messages 40 bytes are sufficient to encode the transmitted information.

LIST_REQUEST_REPLY messages indicate the addresses of the different members of the list of connected peers. They also indicate the source rate and the number of trees. Depending on the size of the list transmitted by the source (i.e., between 1 peer and 55 peers), the size of this packet can vary between 50 and 500 bytes (8 bytes per IP address and 40 bytes for additional information including headers). Instead, we assume a fixed size of 120 bytes. This has little influence on the results we present (as we will see in Sec. 4.2, traffic due to join messages represent 1% of the control protocol, which itself only represents 2-5% of the total traffic).

PROBE_REPLY messages contain their height in the different trees (4 bytes), the available throughput of the peer (this can be encoded with 1 kb/s precision with 10 bits). We assume these packets are 80 bytes long which is more than sufficient.

ATTACH_REPLY messages contain the result of the attachment (1 bit), the tree they belong to (4 bits), the available throughput of the peer (this can be encoded with 1 kb/s precision with 10 bits), and the addresses of peers between the source and them. We assume these packets are 80 bytes long, which leaves enough space for 6 peers. As tree heights typically vary between 1 and 10, in the experiments we present, this is a justifiable approximation.

HELLO messages indicate the tree they are destined to (4 bits), the number of descendants of a peer (2 bytes) and the round-trip time between the peer and the parent (1 byte for round-trip times between 1ms and 256 ms, with 1 ms precision).

HELLO_REPLY messages include the available throughput (10 bits), the tree they are destined to (4 bits), their height in the tree (4 bits), and the addresses of peers between them and the source. These addresses are first sent in the ATTACH_REPLY message; they only need to be transmitted when a change occurs. As this does not occur frequently, we assume both HELLO and HELLO_REPLY messages can be encoded with 40 bytes.

Table 4.2. Sizes of different packet types.

LIST_REQUEST	40 bytes
LIST_REQUEST_REPLY	120 bytes
ATTACH_REQUEST	40 bytes
ATTACH_REPLY	80 bytes
JOIN_REPORT	40 bytes
LEAVE_NOTICE	40 bytes
HELLO	40 bytes
HELLO_REPLY	40 bytes
PROBE	40 bytes
PROBE_REPLY	80 bytes

4.2 Experimental Protocol Evaluation

In this section, we describe the experimental setup used to simulate P2P networks with thousands of peers and present an experimental performance evaluation of the protocol. In the simulations, video traffic is sent over the different multicast trees which are constructed by the protocol. Successive video packets are sent over the different trees in round-robin order. A detailed description of the video streaming protocol will be given in Chapter 5. It is not necessary for the understanding of the results presented in this chapter.

4.2.1 Experimental Setup

Simulated Network

To evaluate the performance of the P2P system we carry out experiments over networks ranging from 10 to 3000 peers simulated in ns-2. The peers, including the source, are randomly selected among all the edge nodes of the network topologies. The backbone links are sufficiently provisioned so that congestion only occurs on the links connecting the peers to the network. The propagation delay over each link is 5 ms. For most of the experiments the diameter of the network is 10 hops; in the cases when the number of participating peers is 75 or less, the diameter of the network is 8 hops. Losses are only due to disconnections or delay, and transmission errors due to the presence of ISP boundaries or potential wireless last-hop links are ignored.

The control and transmission protocol is implemented over the UDP/IP protocol stack and we ignore any NAT or firewall issue which may limit connectivity or drop this type of traffic.

Simulated Host

Peers have heterogeneous but fixed uplink bandwidth which they have measured and know accurately. The bandwidth of the peers reflects today's available ADSL network access technology. The bandwidth distribution is given in Tab. 4.3. It is derived from the findings of [210], which provides an estimate of the bandwidth of hosts connecting to media servers maintained by a leading content delivery network in 2003-2004. The uplink and downlink of the source are assumed to be 1.4 Mb/s.

The degree indicates the number of children that a parent transmitting a 300 kb/s stream can potentially support. Note that more than half of the peers do not have enough throughput to forward the video stream assuming a system with only 1 multicast tree, thereby making them *free-riders* of the system. However, when more trees are used, the video stream is divided into several smaller sub-streams and these peers have enough resources to contribute their uplink to the system and forward part of the data.

Table 4.3. Peer bandwidth distribution. The degree is computed for a 300 kb/s stream.

			Degree			
Downlink	Uplink	Percentage	1 tree	2 trees	3 trees	4 trees
512 kbps	256 kbps	56%	0	1	2	3
3 Mbps	384 kbps	21%	1	2	3	5
1.5 Mbps	896 kbps	9%	2	5	8	11
20 Mbps	2 Mbps	3%	6	13	20	26
20 Mbps	5 Mbps	11%	16	33	50	66

In the experiments, the dynamic behavior of peers is modeled as follows. A flash crowd is simulated by letting all the peers request the video during the first minute of the video session. During the remaining time, peers join and leave the session ungracefully, following a random Poisson process. Peers remain "on" for an average time of 4.5 minutes. To keep the system in steady-state, disconnected peers reconnect to the system after remaining "off" for 30 seconds, on average (disconnections also follow a Poisson process).

4.2.2 Control Protocol Traffic Distribution

The pie chart shown in Fig. 4.15 illustrates the distribution of control traffic when 4 multicast trees carry the video traffic. To facilitate the analysis we group control messages in 4 main categories. Join messages are exchanged when a peer initially connects to the multicast, they represent 1% of the total control traffic. Attachment requests, which include connection or reconnection requests to the multicast trees also make up for 1% of the protocol overhead. The two most important categories are probe messages and hello messages. The balance between these two categories depends on the number of multicast trees. In the example shown in Fig. 4.15, hello messages represent 83% of the control traffic and probe messages 15%. This reflects the stability of the multicast trees, which do not require a large amount of control traffic for maintenance. When the number of trees is larger, the relative proportion of probe messages increases. It reaches 20 % of the overall control traffic for 8 trees. This is largely due to the fact that more parents are queried during the attachment process. We believe the protocol traffic can be further optimized to reduce the hello traffic. The relative proportion of control traffic and video traffic will be discussed in the following.

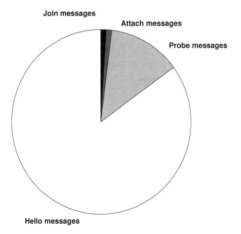

Fig. 4.15. Relative distribution of control traffic. Experiment run for 300 peers on a 1000-node graph. Four multicast trees are maintained by the protocol.

4.2.3 Join and Rejoin Latency

Figure 4.16 shows the cumulative distribution function (CDF) of the join time, i.e., the time necessary for a node to join a multicast tree. The CDF for the rejoin time, i.e., the time a node takes to rejoin a tree once the disconnection of its parent has been detected is also represented. For more than 90% of the peers, joining takes less than 0.7 s. Indeed in most cases, this process can be decomposed into 3 steps: 1 round-trip time to the source to obtain a list of candidate parents (100 ms, on average, for the network on which the simulation is run), waiting for the protocol timer to expire in the probe state (0.5 s), 1 round-trip time to the chosen parent candidate (100 ms, on average). This indicates, that in most cases, at least one of the peers queried during the PROBE state does not have enough available throughput and does not reply to the probe message. This forces the peer to wait for the protocol timer to expire. In a real-life implementation, join and rejoin latencies should also include the time to connect two hosts which might both be behind NATs. As running the protocol STUN [192] to establish such a connection requires less than a second, the joining latency of the system would be comparable to a server-based system which redirects users towards the closest proxy.

Once a peer discovers it has been disconnected from one of the multicast trees, it takes an additional 0.7 s to rejoin, on average. This process is extremely fast 40% of the time, when a peer is able to reconnect to a parent it is already receiving traffic from, on one of the other trees, following the algorithm detailed in Fig. 4.11. In this case, the rejoin time corresponds to one round-trip time to this particular parent (100 ms, on average, for the network used in this simulation), if there is no congestion. The delay increases when a peer needs to request a fresh list of connected peers from the source. In this case, the peer has to go through the join process again, which takes, as seen above, about 0.7 s for the case depicted in Fig. 4.16. In the worse cases, this may occur several times especially since the peer is competing with other disconnected users. This explains the long tail of the CDF.

4.2.4 Scalability

Figure 4.17 illustrates the performance of the protocol in terms of scalability. The aggregate video traffic exchanged between the peers, as well as the control traffic is shown on the left vertical axis. The amount of control overhead is represented on the right vertical axis. Results are collected for a 250 kb/s video stream. In this set of experiments, we use 4 multicast trees and allow no retransmission. As expected, the aggregate video traffic exchanged over the network increases linearly with the number of participating peers. Nevertheless, the percentage of traffic representing control remains constant and represents only between 2 and 3% of the total traffic. This constant overhead shows that the protocol is scalable within the limits of the system. Note that it is difficult to collect results for larger populations due to the implementation of the ns-2 simulator which computes complete, non-hierarchical routing tables at each physical node. The sheer size of these tables significantly slows down the simulations for number of users exceeding 1000.

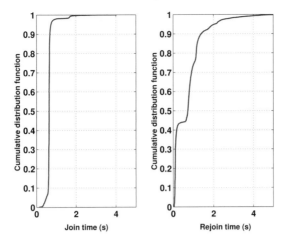

Fig. 4.16. Distribution of the time needed to join a multicast tree (left) and to rejoin a tree after a parent disconnection (right). Experiment run for 300 peers on a 1000-node graph. Four multicast trees are maintained by the protocol. The diameter of the network is 10 hops.

The only centralized part of the protocol is due to traffic exchanged with the source for connection establishment. As discussed above, this fraction of the protocol traffic represents only 1% of the total overhead. For 3000 peers, connection establishment traffic amounts to almost 70 kb/s on both the uplink and the downlink of the source. Hence, for larger populations of peers, a proportional amount of throughput should be reserved at the source to avoid disrupting the video multicast.

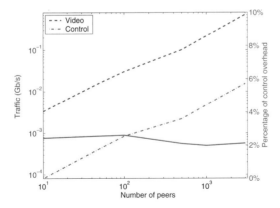

Fig. 4.17. Aggregate traffic for different number of participating peers and control overhead. Results are shown on a logarithmic scale. Figure reprinted, with permission, from [211] © 2006 IEEE.

4.2.5 Limiting Throughput

In this section, we discuss the video rate which can be supported by the P2P network. Our goal is to analyze whether or not stable multicast trees can be built by the protocol when the attachment of each peer requires a given throughput (i.e., the rate indicated by the source during the JOIN process, as illustrated in Fig. 4.2). Unlike in Chapter 5, we do not consider, in this section, whether this throughput is high enough to support a delay-constrained video stream.

The average throughput of the peers needs to be sufficient to support, continually, the connection of other peers on the different multicast trees. In theory, one would expect this to be possible as long as the average throughput of the peers remains above the rate each peer requests to connect to the P2P network. This, however, overlooks the difficulty of not depleting the throughput available to one of the trees, when the number of peers is limited and the available throughput is lower than its statistical average. In order to limit this effect, the resources of the network need to exceed the source rate by a significant margin.

We investigate what is the limiting throughput of the P2P network by observing the variation of the tree sizes as a function of time. We run the experiment for three different source rates: 350 kb/s, 400 kb/s and 450 kb/s. In order to avoid creating any congestion-related artifact the actual rate of the transmitted video stream is set to 164 kb/s in each experiment, which can be easily accomodated by the network. Hence, the only variable parameter is the rate indicated by the source during the JOIN process (350 kb/s, 400 kb/s, and 450 kb/s) which determines the amount of available throughput peers need to construct the multicast trees. Results indicating the structure of the different multicast trees are collected every 3 seconds for 800 seconds, starting 100 seconds after the beginning of the multicast session, after the system has reached steady state. Results are reported for the tree with worst performance (i.e., the one for which variations are most noticeable). Results are shown in Fig. 4.18. When the source rate is 350 kb/s, when 3, 4 or 8 trees are maintained by the protocol, the tree size appears stable. The tree size dips 3 times during the experiment but this occurs for very short periods of time and does not appear on the graphs. When the protocol maintains 2 trees, these dips are more frequent, however, even in this case, the tree size appears stable. For source rates of 400 kb/s, regardless of the number of trees, the frequency of the dips increases. For 2, 4 and 8 trees, there is at least a period during which less than 50 peers are attached to the multicast trees for 10 seconds or more. These events occur even more frequently when the source rate is 450 kb/s. In these two cases, the tree size is much more unstable. The pronounced tree size dips are caused by the disconnection of one of the highest peers of one of the trees, followed by a sequence of reconnections which lead to the absence of peers connected to this tree with enough available throughput to support an additional connection. This "starvation" makes it impossible for peers to join the tree, for long periods of time.

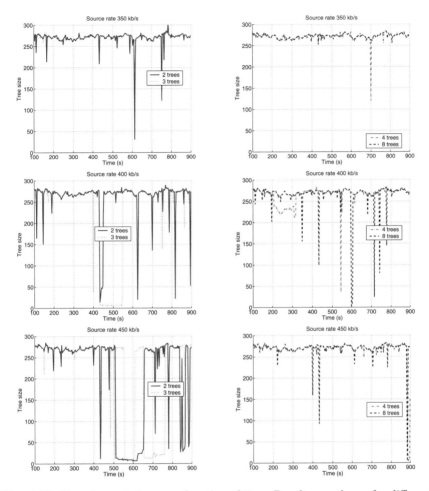

Fig. 4.18. Tree size variation as a function of time. Results are shown for different source rates: 350kb/s (top), 400kb/s (middle), 450kb/s (bottom). Plots on the left represent the results when the protocol maintains either 2 or 3 multicast trees, plots on the right represent the results when the protocol maintains either 4 or 8 multicast trees. In all cases, results are shown for the tree with the worse performance. The video stream sent from the source is 164 kb/s.

This surprising result can be explained as follows. In addition to the requirement that the average uplink throughput of the peer be above the source rate, another condition needs to be satisfied. As the trees are being built, there needs to be, continually, enough available throughput to support at least one extra peer on each of the trees. This requirement is easy to fulfill after each tree reaches a sufficient size, provided the constraint on the average throughput is lax. However, due to the non-homogeneous bandwidth distribution of the peers, it may hamper the initial phases of growth of a tree. This is illustrated in Fig. 4.19, where we assume that the source may support 6 connections but that peers $R1$ to $R5$ can only support 1 connection. In this simple example, no further connection to Tree 2 is possible.

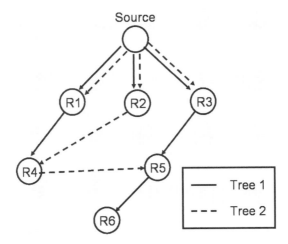

Fig. 4.19. Tree construction failure due to the presence of many low bandwidth peers at the base of the multicast tree.

We explore this effect in more detail by studying a simple model of the tree-building algorithm. We model the growth of the trees as follows: we number the peers and add them to the different trees, successively. When adding peer i to one of the trees, we consider peers 1 (i.e., the source) to $i-1$ consecutively and create a connection to the first peer with available throughput; we then repeat the process for the following tree. If a peer is unable to establish a connection a failure is declared. The model ensures minimum height trees are built. For simplicity, we do not model the diversity criterion which is implemented in the two parent selection algorithms of the protocol, represented in Fig. 4.4 and in Fig. 4.10. Failures only occur in the initial stages of the tree building algorithm (i.e., for less than 30 peers). We collect results for 300 peers, different source rates and different numbers of trees. While collecting results, we run the experiments 5000 times for each point. Results indicating the probability of success of adding the 300 peers to the multicast trees are represented in Fig. 4.20.

While the source rate remains under 256 kb/s, the probability of success is 1. This is not surprising as this corresponds to the smallest uplink bandwidth of the peers. In this case, it is always possible to add a peer. For example, it

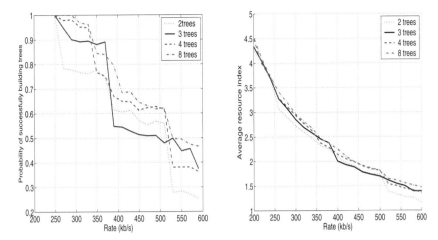

Fig. 4.20. Estimate of the probability of successfully building the multicast trees for different source rates and different numbers of trees (left). The probability is computed by attempting to build 300-peer trees. For each of the 5000 trials conducted, different bandwidths are attributed to the different peers according to the distribution indicated in Tab. 4.3. Average resource index for different source rates and different numbers of trees (right).

is possible to build a connection to the last peer that has joined the network. For rates above 256 kb/s, the probability of successfully building the multicast trees decreases. The curves follow the same trend for different numbers of trees and while the probability of success is usually higher for larger number of trees, this is not always the case. For rates above 400 kb/s the probability of successfully building the multicast trees is under 70%. On the right of Fig. 4.20, we show the resource index of the network of peers for different number of trees and difference source rates. This number is the average degree (as represented, for example, for a source rate of 300 kb/s in Tab. 4.3) divided by the number of trees; in other words, the number of children which can be supported per peer. The resource index does not vary smoothly as a function of rate; in addition, crossings occur between curves representing different number of trees, which indicates that, for some particular rates, throughput usage may be higher for smaller number of trees. The variation of the resource index explains the uneven variation of the probability of successfully building a tree and the crossovers of these different probabilities for different numbers of trees.

As observed in our network experiments, the curves of the model predict that for a given source rate, despite the fact that the average throughput of the peers is sufficient, the probability of successfully building the trees may be significantly lower than 1. This phenomenon is caused by the non-homogeneous bandwidth distribution of the peers which lead to situations where the throughput available to the peers is not sufficient. This occurs when there are very few peers attached to a tree and they mostly have low uplink bandwidth. This is why, when the source rate is above 400 kb/s, when the disconnection of one of the peers close to the source forces the affected tree to be almost entirely rebuilt, the tree construction sometimes fails and many peers are disconnected from the tree for a long period of time. This happens, for example, if a low bandwidth peer joins the top of the tree and accepts as a child one or several peers on another tree. Eventually, peers causing starvation will disconnect and the tree will be rebuilt successfully. Compared to the average uplink throughput of the peers of 914 kb/s, which can be derived from Tab. 4.3, limiting the source rate to between 350 kb/s and 400 kb/s represents an over-provisioning factor between 2.6 and 2.3. This is significantly more than the throughput required for a server-based system and is a limitation of this tree-based P2P protocol. This requirement may be alleviated by actively managing the tree structures to limit the attachment of low bandwidth peers at the base of the tree. This improvement, however, is not incorporated in the version of the protocol used in this book.

4.3 Chapter Summary

A video stream can be forwarded to a large population of peers, without the need of any dedicated infrastructure, by letting the viewers contribute their uplink to relay traffic over application-layer multicast trees. We analyze, in this chapter, the performance of a protocol which lets peers construct and maintain these trees in a distributed fashion. It achieves very good performance in terms of overhead, latency and scalability. Connection or reconnection to the trees require less than 2 s and the overhead of the protocol represents only 2 to 5% of the total exchanged traffic, depending on the number of multicast trees. This is independent of the number of participating peers, within the limits of the simulation system, which lets us consider up to a few thousand peers. To ensure the stability of the trees, the average throughput of the peers should be at least twice the throughput necessary to attach a joining peer to the multicast trees. Otherwise, due to the non-homogeneous bandwidth distribution of the peers, starvation may occur and hamper the initial growth of a tree. When throughput over-provisioning is sufficiently high, the protocol leads to stable distribution structures despite the dynamic behavior of the peers which may disconnect from the session at any time.

5

Video Streaming over a Peer-to-Peer Network

The performance of P2P video streaming systems can be improved by breaking away from the common practice which focuses on designing better control protocols, while ignoring the properties of the transmitted data stream. An alternative is to design adaptive algorithms where encoding and streaming are tailored to the video content and to the network protocol. Although adaptive video encoding and streaming have been studied for a number of years in server-client systems and some of this work was extended to IP multicast, this approach is novel for P2P streaming systems which are still in their infancy. The algorithms we present in this chapter could be used for different P2P control protocols based on multiple multicast trees. In our experiments, we rely on the distributed control protocol presented, in detail, in Chapter 4.

We begin this chapter by describing a simple video streaming protocol which we will improve upon in the second part of the chapter. We describe a low-complexity video scheduler for P2P networks, based on the concept of congestion-distortion optimized scheduling analyzed in Chapter 3. This algorithm is composed of two parts. The first part is a prioritization scheme which is run by the sending peers. This scheme schedules the transmission of video packets destined to multiple peers. It bases its decisions on the unequal contribution of different packets to the overall video distortion. It also takes into account information collected about the structure of the multicast trees, to favor peers with a large set of descendants. Similarly to CoDiO light, it spaces its transmissions to avoid creating congestion on its uplink. The second part is a distortion-optimized retransmission scheduler, run by the receivers to recover missing video packets when they are disconnected from one (several) multicast tree(s). The performance of this hybrid algorithm (part sender, part receiver), denoted by *CoDiO P2P*, is compared to the CoDiO scheduler described in Chapter 3. Finally, in Sec. 5.3, we analyze the performance of these different video streaming techniques, for a simulated network with hundreds of peers.

5.1 Video Streaming Protocol

We assume peers run the control protocol described in Chapter 4 to build different multicast trees rooted at the source. Each peer is an interior node or a leaf in *all* of the different trees, unless it has been disconnected and is trying to reestablish a connection. Peers receive video traffic from their different parents in each of the multicast trees. When one of their parents leaves the session, peers issue retransmission requests to the parents they are still connected to, in order to mitigate losses, while the control protocol seeks a suitable parent to reconnect to.

5.1.1 Video Packet Transmission

The multicast source is responsible for sending the media stream over the different transmission trees. We consider a simple distribution mechanism where video frames are transmitted, following their encoding order, at regular intervals, 30 times per second[1]. After MTU fragmentation, the video frames are sent, packet by packet, over different multicast trees. If the number of trees is denoted by *numTrees*, Packet n is transmitted over Tree n mod *numTrees*. This provides a simple mapping between packet numbers and multicast trees. This mapping is helpful for error resilience, as each peer knows the sequence numbers of the different packets it is supposed to receive over each tree. This balanced distribution mechanism also prevents large rate spikes on the trees which could create congestion.

The multicast source is also responsible for packetizing the media stream, prior to transmission. As video is transmitted to the different peers over multiple paths, out-of-order arrivals are expected. Packet headers are therefore necessary to provide enough information to reconstitute the media stream before decoding. Video packet headers are created by the source; they contain the packet number, the video frame number, the total number of packets in the frame, the place of the particular packet among them and the playout deadline of the packet. Before transmitting a packet on one of the trees, the source will also indicate in its header the sequence number of the previous packet it transmitted over this tree, to facilitate the detection of dropped packets.

When a peer receives a video packet on one of the multicast trees, it immediately forwards it to its descendants on the same tree, as long as it is not past its playout deadline. Before doing so, the peer updates the header of the video packet to indicate the sequence number of the previous packet it sent on the tree.

---

[1] For a video sequence encoded at 30 frames/s.

5.1.2 Retransmissions

When the control protocol detects a parent disconnection, the peer creates a list of missing packets. This list contains the sequence number of all the packets which should have been received over the tree the peer is disconnected from. The range considered extends from the next packet to be decoded, to the highest packet number received on the other multicast trees. To ensure all the missing packets are identified the list of missing packets is refreshed every 100 ms, until the peer has re-established a connection to the missing tree and has received several video packets from this tree.

When packets are dropped, out-of-order arrivals are detected thanks to the information contained in the video header which includes the sequence number of the packet previously sent along the same multicast tree. A peer requests the missing packets which are not past due from its different parents, following the sequence number of the packets. Lower sequence numbers are requested first. This approach benefits from the diversity in the trees built by the control protocol which allows a peer to request retransmissions over alternate paths.

Retransmission requests place additional burden on the uplink of forwarding peers, already responsible for forwarding video packets transmitted over one of the multicast trees. As an outstanding retransmission request represents a packet being transmitted or processed between the two peers, these packets potentially contribute to end-to-end delay, and hence to congestion. The retransmission scheduler limits the congestion created by retransmissions by bounding the number of unacknowledged retransmission requests from a peer to each of its parents. When a retransmission request may be sent to two or more parents, the peer chooses one of them at random. Obviously, retransmission requests are not sent over trees from which the peer is disconnected.

When a parent receives a retransmission request for a packet it has not received, it informs the requesting peer by sending a negative acknowledgment (NACK) back. If it has already received this packet, it is retransmitted immediately. The exact time at which a retransmission reply will be received by the peer depends on the state of the bottleneck queue of its parent, on its uplink throughput and on future packet arrivals. Therefore it cannot be estimated precisely. A retransmission request is assumed to be lost if it has not been acknowledged or if no reply has been received in the following 200 ms. In our simulation setup, the average forward trip time is 50 ms, therefore, 200 ms is sufficient to obtain a retransmitted packet as packet sizes are smaller or equal to MTUs.

5.2 Peer-to-Peer CoDiO Scheduling

In this section, we analyze the benefits of packet scheduling for P2P networks. The schedulers CoDiO and CoDiO light presented in Chapter 3, perform optimized scheduling of video in a server-client scenario and achieve significant performance gains compared to a content-oblivious sequential scheduler. However, neither CoDiO nor CoDiO light is well-suited to P2P video streaming. A new type of scheduler, based on the ideas developed in Chapter 3, is needed in this scenario.

First, CoDiO and CoDiO light assume the server has extensive knowledge of the rate-distortion properties of the video streaming being sent to the receiver. For P2P streaming, clients which join the multicast also relay the video stream. We cannot assume these hosts have access to detailed information on the stream they are forwarding. Although the source of the multicast could have access to this type of data, it would be impractical to transmit it to the large number of peers of the session which schedule video packets.

A second impediment is that our video streaming protocol does not include acknowledgments. When the channel is prone to losses, both CoDiO and CoDiO light rely on acknowledgments (ACKs), sent from the client for each transmitted packet, to refine their estimates of the set of received packets. ACKs are important to compute accurate expected distortion. This was studied, for example, in [77, 212], for RaDiO. In P2P streaming, sending acknowledgments will reduce the uplink throughput of the clients, which, in this case, is used to forward video packets to other peers. If we assume the size of an acknowledgment packet to be approximately 40 bytes, this results in 9.6 kb/s of traffic, when video is sent at 30 frames per second. For the sequence *Foreman*, encoded at 257 kb/s, when the video is transmitted packet by packet because of MTU packetization, the ACK traffic rate reaches 15 kb/s. This should be avoided as it would more than double the rate of control traffic which represents only a few percent of the video traffic exchanged, as analyzed in Chapter 4.

Finally, P2P video streaming also requires very low complexity. Indeed, peers with high uplink throughput may forward video to more than a dozen peers. For CoDiO, this would increase the search space exponentially. For CoDiO light, the number of schedules to compare would scale up linearly. As we cannot assume that peers are dedicated to forwarding video packets and may be simultaneously running other applications, this may increase the CPU requirement for these peers beyond an acceptable level. In addition, because of the computational constraints of our experimental environment, the scheduler should be simple enough to simulate hundreds of peers, all simultaneously scheduling video packets, on *one* Pentium 4, clocked at 2.8 GHz, with 1 GB of memory.

Extending CoDiO light to P2P requires considering several new problems which characterize the particular nature of this transmission scenario. Unlike unicast, each peer receives video packets from a set of senders and forwards them to several receivers. This raises a number of interesting questions. How can a peer implement an adaptive forwarding transmission scheme and yet coordinate its scheduling policies with other senders forwarding video packets to the same descendant? Which of its different descendants should a peer favor when its resources are insufficient to serve them all?

In the next two sections (Sec. 5.2.1 and Sec. 5.2.2), we describe a low-complexity scheduling scheme, which we denote by *CoDiO P2P*, which builds on the ideas developed in Chapter 3. This algorithm is composed of two parts:

- At the sender, a prioritization scheme schedules the transmission of video packets destined to multiple peers. It bases its decisions on the unequal contribution of different packets to the overall video distortion. It also takes into account information collected about the structure of the multicast trees, to favor peers with a large set of descendants. Similarly to CoDiO light, it spaces its transmissions to avoid creating congestion on its uplink.
- At the receiver, we describe a distortion-optimized algorithm to recover missing video packets when a peer is disconnected from one (or several) multicast tree(s).

In Sec. 5.2.3, the performance of CoDiO P2P is compared to the CoDiO scheduler described in Chapter 3.

5.2.1 Sender-Driven Prioritization

Relaying traffic over the uplink of the peers may lead to congestion on the multi-hop path separating the source from any particular peer. In particular, because the rate of a video stream often varies or because of unexpected retransmission requests, a peer may sometimes lack the resources to forward all the data expected by its descendants. Scheduling can help maintain video quality in the instances when a peer has to drop some packets to ensure timely delivery of the more significant portion of the video. The prioritization algorithm determines iteratively which is the next most important packet by comparing the importance of each queued packet.

For Packet n the importance, $\tilde{D}(n)$, is computed as a function of the video frame type and of the order in the GOP. This quantity reflects the sensitivity of the video quality to the reception of the packet. As peers do not collect detailed rate-distortion information about the stream they are transmitting and as the exact state of the reception buffer of their descendants is not known either, this sensitivity needs to be approximated. We choose to express $\tilde{D}(n)$ as the number of frames which will be affected if the frame Packet n belongs to is not decoded correctly.

Figure 5.1 shows the importance $\tilde{D}(n)$ of different frames for an open encoding structure with periodic I frames. The importance of an I frame is 19, as its loss would affect the 16-frame GOP as well as the 3 preceding B frames. The importance of the different P frames is 15, 11 and 7, depending on their place in the GOP, and the importance of each B frame is 1. In the P2P multicast scenario, CoDiO P2P schedules video streams packet by packet, rather than frame by frame; in this case, the importance of a packet corresponds to the importance of the frame it belongs to. In addition, packets or frames are only considered by the scheduler as long as they are not past their playout deadline. The algorithm does not, otherwise, take playout deadlines or delay into account.

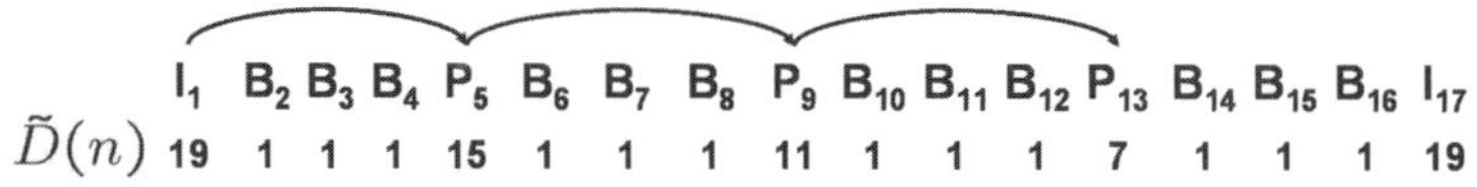

$$\overbrace{\text{I}_1 \quad \text{B}_2 \ \text{B}_3 \ \text{B}_4 \ \text{P}_5} \ \overbrace{\text{B}_6 \ \text{B}_7 \ \text{B}_8 \ \text{P}_9} \ \overbrace{\text{B}_{10} \ \text{B}_{11} \ \text{B}_{12} \ \text{P}_{13}} \ \text{B}_{14} \ \text{B}_{15} \ \text{B}_{16} \ \text{I}_{17}$$

$\tilde{D}(n)$	19	1	1	1	15	1	1	1	11	1	1	1	7	1	1	1	19

Fig. 5.1. Periodic encoding structure showing the importance of different frames. The numbering reflects the display order of the pictures.

The role of the scheduler is not only to determine in which order to send packets destined to a particular peer, but also, how to prioritize among the different descendants of a peer. Therefore, the importance of each packet should also be adjusted to the number of descendants in the multicast tree that would be affected by the loss or late arrival of this packet. Hence, the scheduler should adapt its decisions to the video content *and* to the structure of the underlying multicast trees.

Our prioritization algorithm determines iteratively which is the next most important packet by comparing the *impact* of each queued packet. For a Packet n, addressed to Peer m, the impact is expressed as:

$$I(n, m) = \tilde{D}(n) * (NumDescendants(m) + 1) \tag{5.1}$$

In (5.1), $NumDescendants(m)$ represents the number of peers to which Packet n will be forwarded after reaching Peer m, this information is collected by the control protocol, described in Chapter 4, when "hello" packets are exchanged between neighboring peers to maintain the multicast trees. $\tilde{D}(n)$ is the importance we have just described.

Similarly to CoDiO light presented in Chapter 3, the prioritization algorithm spaces successive transmissions to ensure congestion is not created on the bottleneck link of the network path. In this case, the bottleneck is the uplink of the forwarding peer, which we assume not to be shared with other applications. Controlling the size of the queue of this link is, therefore, straightforward. Transmissions are spaced based on the time needed for the previous video packet to traverse the uplink. In addition, a small fraction of the link throughput is reserved to account for control traffic. This is sufficient to limit the delay of control packets. In our simulations, 20 kb/s of throughput is set aside for this purpose regardless of the uplink bandwidth of the peer. Please also note that when a packet retransmission is requested by a descendant of the peer, the importance of the retransmission packet is computed according to (5.1). Therefore, the scheduler does not systematically favor retransmitted packets.

5.2.2 Distortion-Optimized Retransmission Scheduling

To improve the retransmission scheme described in Sec. 5.1, we suggest a distortion-optimized approach similar to that described in Chapter 3 to request, in priority, the most important missing packets from the parents of the peer, when it is partially disconnected from the multicast session. Different from the CoDiO scheduler of Chapter 3, which is run by the video source, the algorithm presented in this section is run by receivers which do not know in advance the rate-distortion properties of the frames they will receive. Therefore the distortion contribution of missing packets to the overall video quality needs to be estimated.

Missing Frames

The information present in the headers of received video packets includes packet numbers which makes missing packets easy to identify following a parent disconnection. However, it is important to relate the missing packets to missing video frames in order to estimate which are the most critical in terms of video quality. A list of missing frames is first determined by forming an estimated mapping between missing packets and their corresponding frame using additional information contained in the header of received video packets (packet number, frame number, number of packets in the frame, etc.). For this purpose we use Algorithm 5.2.1, which estimates the frame number of a missing packet, n. In Algorithm 5.2.1, each frame is a associated with a variable denoted by *initialized* which indicates whether a packet for this frame has been received. If it has, then the sequence number of the packets composing the frame is known, and in particular, the $first\_packet$ and the $last\_packet$ of the frame. The $current\_frame$, is the frame displayed by the peer. In our simulations we use $history\_window = 64$ frames. The idea of the algorithm is to find upper and lower bounds for the frame number corresponding to Packet n. If during the process the frame number is not determined, the average between the upper and lower bound is returned.

Algorithm 5.2.1: MapPacketToFrame(n)

comment: First, find an upper bound for the frame number.

$upper\_bound \leftarrow current\_frame$
while ($upper\_bound \leq current\_frame + history\_window$)
$\quad$ **do** $\begin{cases} \textbf{if } (upper\_bound.initialized) \\ \quad \textbf{then } \begin{cases} \textbf{if } (upper\_bound.first\_packet > n) \\ \quad \textbf{then } break \\ \textbf{else if } (upper\_bound.first\_packet \leq n \leq \\ \qquad\qquad\qquad upper\_bound.last\_packet) \\ \quad \textbf{then return } (upper\_bound) \end{cases} \\ upper\_bound \leftarrow upper\_bound + 1 \end{cases}$

comment: Then, find a lower bound for the frame number.

$lower\_bound \leftarrow upper\_bound$
while $lower\_bound > current\_frame$
$\quad$ **do** $\begin{cases} \textbf{if } (lower\_bound.initialized) \\ \quad \textbf{then } \begin{cases} \textbf{if } (lower\_bound.last\_packet < n) \\ \quad \textbf{then } break \end{cases} \\ lower\_bound \leftarrow lower\_bound - 1 \end{cases}$
if ($upper\_bound.initialized$ **and** $upper\_bound.first\_packet - 1 == n$)
$\quad$ **then return** ($upper\_bound - 1$)
$\quad$ **else if** ($lower\_bound.initialized$ **and** $lower\_bound.last\_packet + 1 == n$)
$\quad$ **then return** ($lower\_bound + 1$)
$\quad$ **else**
$\quad$ **then return** ($\lfloor \frac{lower\_bound + upper\_bound}{2} \rfloor$)

Distortion Estimation

The scheduler uses its knowledge of the GOP structure to determine which missing frame has the highest contribution to the total expected distortion. Our approach is to estimate the decoded video distortion which would be obtained if one of the different missing frames was retransmitted successfully.

We assume that previous frame concealment is used, as described in Appendix A, and that when a frame is lost the displayed picture is frozen until the next decodable frame. Given a set of received frames, one of the missing frames, k, and the encoding structure of the video, the scheduler constructs a function $c_k(s)$ which indicates, based on the state of the current decoder buffer, which frame will be shown at the time Frame s is due, if Frame k is successfully recovered. As in Chapter 3, we let $D(s, c_k(s))$ denote the distortion resulting from showing Frame $c_k(s)$ instead of Frame s. Each display outcome is associated with the appropriate distortion value and the resulting video quality is computed over several frames (in our simulations, the two following GOPs):

$$D_k = \sum_{i=1}^{n} D(s_i, c_k(s_i)) \qquad (5.2)$$

The most important frame to request for retransmission is simply the frame which minimizes the decoded distortion:

$$k^* = Argmin_k D_k \qquad (5.3)$$

Retransmission requests are sent out, packet by packet, in order of importance, according to this metric.

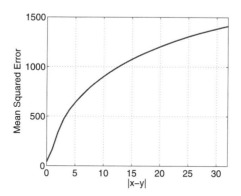

Fig. 5.2. Estimated distortion as a function of the proximity of the frame used for concealment. The encoding rate for the different sequences used to derive this average is as follows. Container: 327 kb/s, Foreman: 339 kb/s, Mobile: 306 kb/s, Mother & Daughter: 319 kb/s, News: 319 kb/s, Salesman: 311 kb/s.

As the peers do not know the exact properties of the video sequence they are receiving, we estimate $D(x, y)$ by a function $D_{est}(x, y)$, computed by averaging the results from different sequences and stored at each of the peers. $D_{est}(x, y)$ only depends on the difference $x - y$ and captures the increase in terms of MSE resulting from using a frame which is farther away for concealment. This distortion function is shown in Fig. 5.2. It is obtained by taking the average of $D(x, y)$, for $|x - y| < 32$, for all $0 \le x \le 287$ and $0 \le y \le 287$, for the 6 sequences used throughout this book. The sequences are encoded using the GOP structure illustrated in Fig. 5.1. The encoding rate for the different sequences is indicated in the caption of the figure.

5.2.3 Scheduler Evaluation

In this section, we evaluate CoDiO P2P, the hybrid algorithm we have just described, which combines the prioritization scheme run by sending peers and the distortion-optimized retransmission request scheduler run by receivers. We begin the analysis by comparing the performance of CoDiO P2P with CoDiO, the scheduler analyzed in Chapter 3, which picks the best schedule among a large set of schedules selected at random. This comparison is run for a unicast scenario, with one sender and one receiver.

Experimental Setup

The experimental setup is the same as the one used in Chapter 3. We study the performance of the scheduler for a network path with two hops, simulated in ns-2. The first hop is a lossless high-bandwidth duplex 47.5 Mb/s T3 link which is filled with a 22 Mb/s flow of exponential cross traffic. When generating cross traffic, the size of average traffic bursts is 30 kbytes. The second hop is a 400 kb/s link. We consider a fixed packet loss rate of 2% over this link. The total propagation delay over the channel is 52 ms.

For CoDiO, we keep the settings used in Chapter 3. For CoDiO P2P, as this is a unicast scenario we do not consider several multicast trees. The sender uses the prioritization scheme described in Sec. 5.2.1, and spaces its transmissions to according to the 400 kb/s rate of its uplink. The receiver requests retransmissions when it detects out-of-order arrivals. The number of simultaneous unacknowledged retransmission requests is limited to 4, as this was found to maximize performance. We present results for the case when CoDiO P2P transmits video, frame by frame and packet by packet. Please note that because of complexity, CoDiO is unable to optimize schedules for a packetized video stream satisfactorily. It is, hence, limited to transmitting entire frames.

Results are presented for six video sequences compressed using the coding structure depicted in Fig. 5.1. The encoding rate for the different sequences is as follows, Container: 327 kb/s, Foreman: 290 kb/s, Mobile: 342 kb/s, Mother & Daughter: 319 kb/s, News: 358 kb/s, Salesman: 364 kb/s. Sequences are looped 40 times when collecting experimental results. When a packet arrives at the receiver after its playout deadline, the frame it belongs to is discarded as if it were lost. In this case, the frame is concealed using previous frame concealment, as described in detail in Appendix A. As in Chapter 3, the results collected are the sender's transmission rate, the decoded video quality, measured in PSNR and computed as explained in Appendix A, and the congestion (i.e., the average end-to-end delay).

Performance comparison of CoDiO vs. CoDiO P2P

Results in Fig. 5.3, Fig. 5.4, and Fig. 5.5, show the performance of the CoDiO scheduler compared to the CoDiO P2P scheduler in terms of video quality, rate and congestion. Two curves are shown for CoDiO P2P, depending on whether the scheduler sends video frames frame by frame or packet by packet.

When CoDiO P2P schedules entire video frames, despite its simplicity, its performance remains within 2 dB of CoDiO. The performance gap is a consequence of CoDiO P2P not using any delay distribution model and sending and retransmitting frames as long as they are not past their playout deadline. Therefore, the rate for CoDiO P2P decreases less than for CoDiO as the playout deadline is reduced. CoDiO P2P does not always pick the right frames to transmit or retransmit and the performance is lower. However, the congestion created over the link is lower than for CoDiO since CoDiO P2P can never send frames back-to-back.

When CoDiO P2P schedules video frames, packet by packet, its performance is as good or even better than CoDiO. Since it can retransmit smaller portions of a frame, the rate for this scheduler is slightly lower as illustrated in Fig. 5.4. As long as the playout deadline is larger than 600 ms, both CoDiO and CoDiO P2P achieve maximum performance, for most of the sequences. For lower playout deadline, CoDiO does not have time to retransmit I frames, however, because CoDiO P2P operates on a per-packet basis, it can maintain its performance for a longer range. The performance of CoDiO P2P in terms of congestion is excellent, as illustrated in Fig. 5.4. CoDiO P2P spaces its transmission and does not send more than an MTU size packet at a time.

Performance of the retransmission scheduler of CoDiO P2P

Results in Fig. 5.6, show the difference in performance when retransmission packets are requested in a distortion-optimized fashion or are requested sequentially, according to their sequence number. In both cases, the sender performs prioritized scheduling as described in Sec. 5.2.1. The gains for using distortion-optimized retransmission scheduling are modest. They occur for intermediate playout deadlines, when there is not enough time to request all the missing packets. In this case, it is an advantage to request retransmission of the most important packets first. Except for the sequence *Foreman* where there is no gain, the performance improvement is 0.5 dB.

As an additional comment, since the performance peaks for a small number of simultaneous retransmission requests (4 in this case), the scheduler used at the sender is not powerful enough to schedule efficiently the transmission of all the missing packets as well as that of the other video packets. This is because the scheduler only refers to the encoding structure to determine the impact of a packet and does not make use of the playout deadline nor the delay distribution.

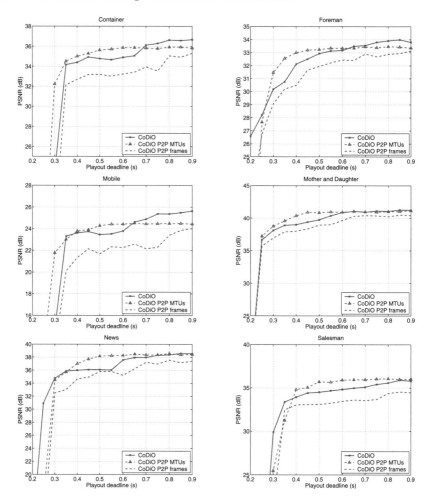

Fig. 5.3. Video quality of CoDiO compared to CoDiO P2P for frame-by-frame transmission and for packet-by-packet transmission. The encoding rate for the different sequences is as follows, Container: 327 kb/s, Foreman: 290 kb/s, Mobile: 342 kb/s, Mother & Daughter: 319 kb/s, News: 358 kb/s, Salesman: 364 kb/s.

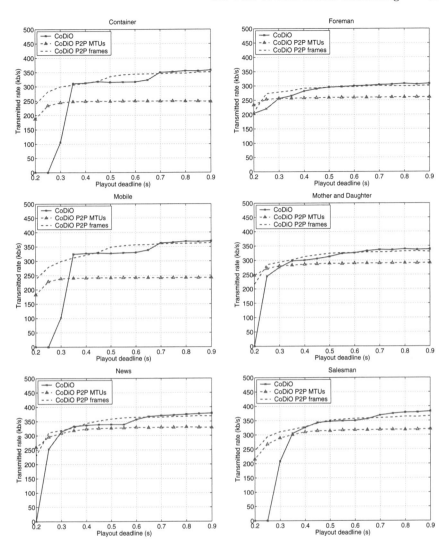

Fig. 5.4. Transmitted rate of CoDiO compared to CoDiO P2P for frame-by-frame transmission and for packet-by-packet transmission. The encoding rate for the different sequences is as follows, Container: 327 kb/s, Foreman: 290 kb/s, Mobile: 342 kb/s, Mother & Daughter: 319 kb/s, News: 358 kb/s, Salesman: 364 kb/s.

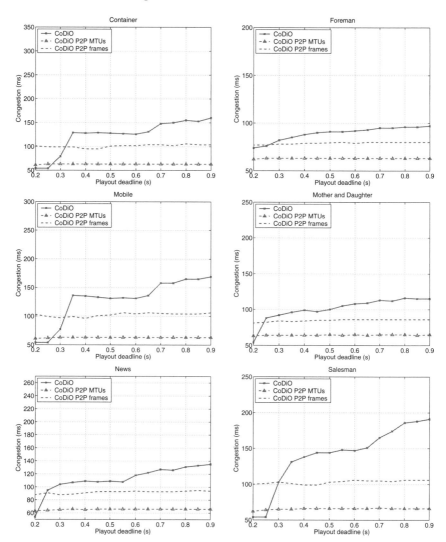

Fig. 5.5. Congestion of CoDiO compared to CoDiO P2P for frame-by-frame transmission and for packet-by-packet transmission. The encoding rate for the different sequences is as follows, Container: 327 kb/s, Foreman: 290 kb/s, Mobile: 342 kb/s, Mother & Daughter: 319 kb/s, News: 358 kb/s, Salesman: 364 kb/s.

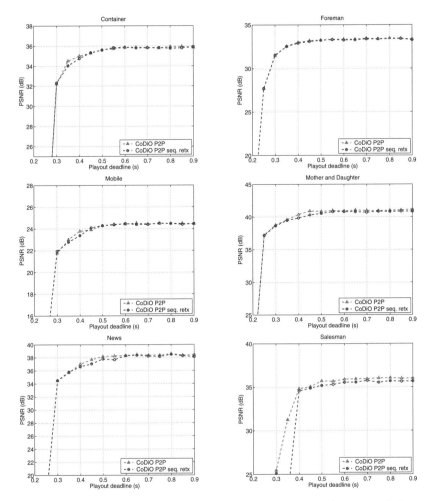

Fig. 5.6. Performance of CoDiO P2P for distortion-optimized retransmission requests and content-oblivious sequential retransmissions. The encoding rate for the different sequences is as follows. Container: 244 kb/s, Foreman: 257 kb/s, Mobile: 237 kb/s, Mother & Daughter: 282 kb/s, News: 319 kb/s, Salesman: 311 kb/s.

5.3 Experimental Results

The simulation setup used for this section is described in detail in Sec 4.2.1, in Chapter 4. This setup is used to simulate a realistic network of hundreds of dynamic peers which serves to evaluate the performance of the P2P system.

5.3.1 Video Sessions

We collect results for the 6 sequences used throughout this book, encoded with H.264 between 250 and 340 kb/s. These 10-second video clips are looped to obtain 30 minute multicast sessions. When packets miss their playout deadline they are discarded by the peers. As described in Appendix A, video decoding errors are concealed by freezing the last correctly decoded video frame until the next decodable frame. Video quality is recorded at the different peers and serves as the main evaluation metric. It is computed during the time the peers are connected to the session. To avoid biases due to transient behavior, we exclude the first 100 seconds of the experiments, when computing average video quality.

The video coding structure is that described in Fig. 5.1. In most cases, the video source transmits video traffic over 4 multicast trees and experiments are run with a playout deadline of 2 seconds.

5.3.2 Diversity

The results shown in Fig. 5.7 illustrate the benefits of using multiple multicast trees. The video quality averaged over the 300 peers is reported on the left vertical axis, and the percentage of control traffic exchanged on the network for different number of trees is reported on the right vertical axis. The latter is computed by taking the ratio between the amount of control traffic on the network and the total amount of traffic (composed of video and control traffic, as there is no cross traffic). Please note that control traffic is also analyzed in more detail in Chapter 4.

In this experiment, the encoding structure illustrated in Fig. 5.1 is used to compress the video. The encoding rate for the different sequences is indicated in the caption of the figure. The peers run the video streaming protocol described in Sec. 5.1 to forward the video packets. Missing packets are requested sequentially and simultaneous retransmission requests are limited to 2 per parent. The aggregate amount of available throughput requested by the peers to join the multicast is 350 kb/s (i.e., 350 kb/s per tree for 1 tree, 175 kb/s per tree for 2 trees, etc.). As explained in Chapter 4 this rate leads to stable multicast trees. In addition, the playout deadline for all the peers is fixed at 2.0 s, which, for our system, is not a stringent constraint.

As the number of trees increases, although the total rate necessary to transmit the entire compressed video remains constant, the rate of the video sub-streams forwarded along each tree decreases linearly. Hence, the amount of free uplink bandwidth required to support an additional child on any particular tree is smaller; this finer granularity leads to better use of the available network bandwidth. In this experiment, the network cannot achieve good performance with only 1 multicast tree. In this case, as indicated in Tab. 4.3, more than half of the peers are free-riders, as their uplink does not allow them to forward the video stream. As a result, many peers are not able to connect to the multicast trees. This causes control traffic to increase as probe messages are exchanged for longer periods, it also decreases the amount of video traffic exchanged, as unconnected peers do not receive the streams and do not forward them. This explains why the control overhead is so high. For 2 or more trees, finer granularity leads to additional available uplink resources. In particular, there are no more free-riders and the available resources are sufficient to sustain high video quality. This is the prevalent factor in determining a suitable number of trees. The results in Fig. 5.7 show that when more multicast trees are used, the control traffic needed to build and maintain the trees increases linearly. In addition, the increased frequency of parent disconnections causes more losses which results in a slightly lower video quality when no retransmissions are allowed. A high video quality can, however, be maintained by using retransmissions.

These results are further analyzed in Fig. 5.8 which shows the percentage of lost frames for the same experiment. The percentage of frozen frames is very high when there is only one tree, as the protocol is not able to maintain a stable multicast tree when there are many free-riders. In the absence of retransmissions, the percentage of frozen frames increases as a function of the number of trees. As expected, this increase is approximately linear, as the frequency of parent disconnections increases on average linearly with the number of trees.

5.3.3 CoDiO P2P

Distortion-Optimized Retransmission Scheduling

We first study the influence of retransmission scheduling on the decoded video quality. Specifically, we analyze to what extent retransmissions mitigate the quality degradation which occurs when the parent of a peer leaves. To illustrate this particular aspect of the system we choose the following scenario. We let 300 peers join the multicast and remain connected. When a steady state is reached, a host close to the source is disconnected. In this experiment, 4 multicast trees are used to transmit the video and the maximum number of unacknowledged retransmission requests on each tree is 2. The performance is shown for 2 video sequences in Fig. 5.9 and in Fig. 5.10, as a function of time, in terms of the video quality. The average video quality is taken over all 299 connected peers. The percentage of peers connected to all 4 trees is also recorded and shown on the right of the figure. The rate for the two sequences is 282 kb/s and 306 kb/s, respectively. The cumulative amount of available

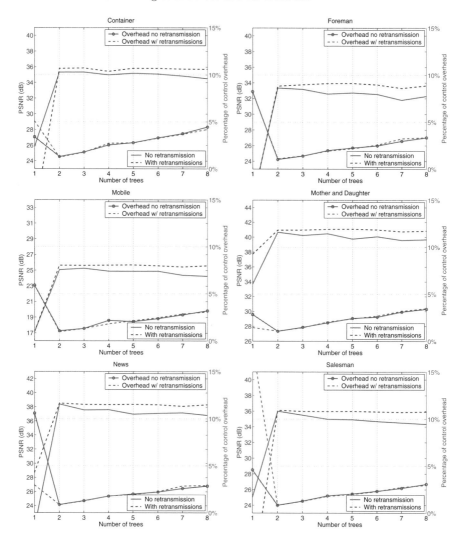

Fig. 5.7. Decoded video quality and overhead for P2P video streaming over different numbers of multicast trees. The encoding rate for the sequences is as follows. Container: 283 kb/s, Foreman: 290 kb/s, Mobile: 306 kb/s, Mother & Daughter: 282 kb/s, News: 319 kb/s, Salesman: 311 kb/s.

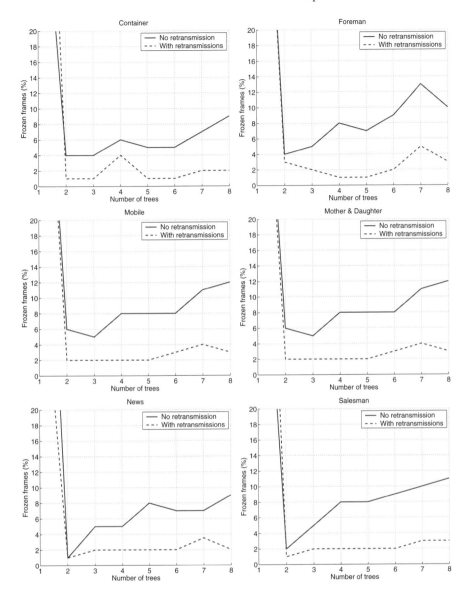

Fig. 5.8. Percentage of frozen frames for different numbers of multicast trees. The encoding rate for the sequences is as follows. Container: 283 kb/s, Foreman: 290 kb/s, Mobile: 306 kb/s, Mother & Daughter: 282 kb/s, News: 319 kb/s, Salesman: 311 kb/s.

throughput requested by the peers to join the multicast is 350 kb/s. The playout deadline for all the peers is fixed to 2.0 s. We compare the retransmission request scheduling of CoDiO P2P to the case where no retransmission is allowed. Results are also shown for the case where retransmission requests for missing packets are issued sequentially, according to their decoding deadline. For all three cases shown in Fig. 5.9 and in Fig. 5.10, at the sender, the scheduler described in Sec. 5.2.1 performs prioritized scheduling between the different queued packets, and only the retransmission method employed by receivers changes.

The host disconnection occurs at time 0, and takes about 1 s to be detected. This can be deduced from the graphs, as connectivity is reported directly by the peers. As illustrated in Fig. 5.9 and in Fig. 5.10, about 40% of the hosts, in one case, and 25%, in the other, are affected by the disconnection. At time 4 s, all the affected peers have recovered. Similar behavior is observed with and without retransmissions and differences are due to the various traffic patterns resulting from different retransmission policies. The video quality during the rejoin time, however, is very different for the three cases. For CoDiO P2P, the video quality remains almost constant over time, as a large majority of missing frames which contribute significantly to decoded video distortion are recovered. As a comparison, for the results shown in Fig. 5.9, the quality drops during the reconnection time by approximately 6 dB when no retransmission are allowed and by 1 dB for the content-oblivious retransmission scheduler. For the results shown in Fig. 5.10, the overall video quality degradation is less severe as the disconnection affects fewer peers. However, due to the motion of the sequence, missing even a B frame leads to a PSNR drop. The quality loss is reduced by half with CoDiO P2P compared to the content-oblivious retransmission scheme and by more than half compared to the case with no retransmission.

Table 5.1 shows the average decoded video quality obtained as the maximum number of unacknowledged retransmission packets per parent is varied. Results are collected for 6 sequences. In this experiment there are 300 peers and video is transmitted over four multicast trees. The playout deadline is fixed to 2.0 s. The encoding structure illustrated in Fig. 5.1 is used to compress the video.

The numbers reported in the table show the gain in terms of average video quality which can be achieved through the use of retransmissions. As illustrated, with one or two simultaneous retransmission requests per tree, gains reach 1.2 dB on average. In addition, we stress that the impact of visual quality, is much larger. The small performance gap is due to the fact that during the 30-minute multicast, the number of disconnections affecting each peer is limited. This is further confirmed by the low percentage of frozen frames which is reported in Tab. 5.2. The performance degrades slightly for 8 retransmissions. This indicates the scheduler at the sender is overwhelmed by the number of packets and does not efficiently prioritize traffic. As previously noted in Sec. 5.2.3, the fact that the performance peaks for a small number

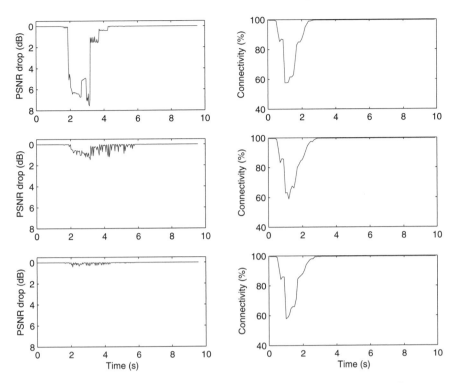

Fig. 5.9. Video quality drop and percentage of peers connected to all 4 trees for no retransmission (top), content-oblivious retransmissions (middle), distortion-optimized retransmissions (bottom). Results shown for the video sequence *Mother and Daughter*.

of simultaneous retransmission requests shows that the scheduler used at the sender is not powerful enough to handle the transmission of all the missing packets in addition to the other video packets. This is, due to the fact that the scheduler only refers to the encoding structure to determine the impact of a packet and does not make use of the playout deadline nor of the transmission delay between the peers.

Throughput Over-Provisioning

As discussed in Chapter 3, throughput over-provisioning is necessary for low-latency streaming, especially for sequences where the instantaneous rate tends to vary. We study this effect in the P2P setting and analyze the influence of scheduling on over-provisioning in this section. We run an experiment where the cumulative amount of available throughput requested by the peers to join the multicast is 350 kb/s and we observe the decoded quality resulting from streaming video encoded at different rates. In this experiment, the encoding

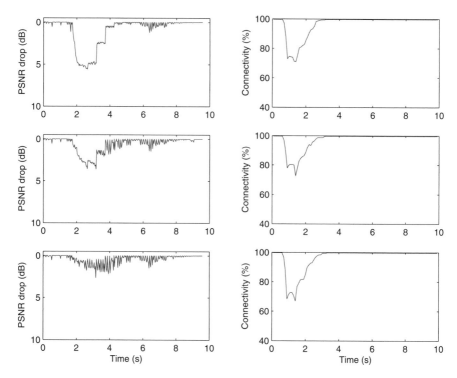

Fig. 5.10. Video quality drop and percentage of peers connected to all 4 trees for no retransmission (top), content-oblivious retransmissions (middle), distortion-optimized retransmissions (bottom). Results shown for the video sequence *Mobile*.

structure illustrated in Fig. 5.1 is used to compress the video. Results are shown in Fig. 5.11, for different playout deadlines, for CoDiO P2P and for the sequential scheduler described in Sec. 5.1. For this second scheduler retransmission requests for missing packets are issued sequentially, according to the packet sequence number. Results show the decoded video quality, averaged over the 300 peers, the horizontal axis shows the rate at which the video is encoded. In this experiment 4 multicast trees are used to carry video traffic.

When the playout deadline is not too stringent (1.4 s, in this experiment) no over-provisioning is necessary. Indeed, for all the sequences, except for *Container*, the video quality is close to the maximal video quality, as long as the encoding rate remains below 350 kb/s. In this case the number of frames lost to frame freezes is only around 2%. When the encoding rate exceeds 350 kb/s, the peers need to forward video packets at a rate which exceeds the throughput reserved for their descendants. In this case, although the average available throughput on the network is well above 350 kb/s[2], the uplink of some of the peers will be overwhelmed by video traffic which explains the

---

[2] The average throughput of the peers is 914 kb/s; it can be derived from Tab. 4.3.

Table 5.1. Average decoded video quality for different numbers of retransmissions. For each sequence, the best result is shown in bold. The encoding rate for the sequences is as follows. Container: 283 kb/s, Foreman: 290 kb/s, Mobile: 306 kb/s, Mother & Daughter: 282 kb/s, News: 311 kb/s, Salesman: 319 kb/s.

Simultaneous retransmissions per tree	PSNR (dB)					
	Container	Foreman	Mobile	M.&D.	News	Salesman
0	35.1	33.35	23.59	39.83	37.5	34.99
1	36.41	33.9	25.62	40.91	**38.4**	35.92
2	**36.44**	**33.94**	**25.75**	**40.97**	37.85	**35.94**
3	36.4	33.92	25.67	40.92	38.41	35.79
8	36.38	33.89	25.73	40.6	38.15	35.86

Table 5.2. Percentage of frozen frames. For each sequence, the best result is shown in bold. The encoding rate for the sequences is as follows. Container: 283 kb/s, Foreman: 290 kb/s, Mobile: 306 kb/s, Mother & Daughter: 282 kb/s, News: 311 kb/s, Salesman: 319 kb/s.

Simultaneous retransmissions per tree	Frozen frames					
	Container	Foreman	Mobile	M.&D.	News	Salesman
0	4%	8%	17%	8%	6%	8%
1	1%	2%	2%	3%	**2%**	3%
2	**1%**	**1%**	**1%**	2%	4%	**2%**
3	1%	2%	2%	2%	2%	3%
8	1%	2%	1%	3%	3%	3%

dip in performance for all the sequences. When the playout deadline is tighter (1.0 s, in this experiment), over-provisioning is necessary as can be seen by the performance degradation for the sequential scheduler which happens at lower rates. This is in line with the results reported in Chapter 3. Again, we stress that the average available throughput on the network is well above 350 kb/s, but congestion may occur on any path linking the source of the multicast to one of the peers. This effect dominates and leads to degraded performance. The effect of congestion is most severe for the sequence *Foreman*. This is due to the instantaneous rate variation which are more significant for this sequence, as illustrated in the curves shown in Appendix A. Again, this is in line with the results presented in Chapter 3. For a playout deadline of 1.0 s, the use of CoDiO P2P reduces the need for over-provisioning. For all the sequences, except for *Foreman* the performance is within 0.5 dB of the maximum performance. CoDiO P2P drops the least important frames when congestion occurs. In this case, the number of frame freezes for the different peers is around 3% or 4%. This is sufficient to maintain high video quality.

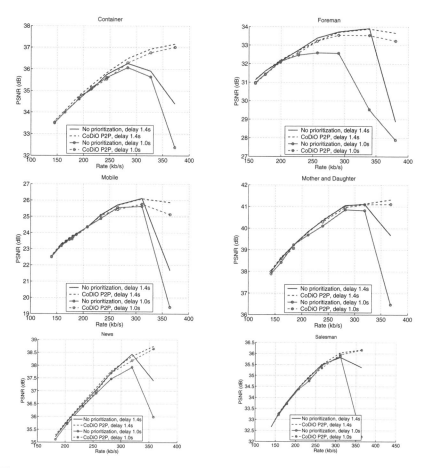

Fig. 5.11. Rate-distortion performance of CoDiO P2P and of the to a non-prioritized sequential scheduler for different encoding rates.

Another type of over-provisioning is also necessary to ensure stability of the trees built by the protocol. This is discussed and analyzed in Chapter 4.

Influence of the Playout Deadline

We analyze further the benefits of CoDiO P2P by studying its performance as a function of the playout deadline. We compare the optimized scheduler to the simpler scheduler described in Sec. 5.1. The results presented in Fig. 5.12 are for a network of 75 peers. In this experiment, the encoding structure illustrated in Fig. 5.1 is used to compress the video. The encoding rate for the sequences is indicated in the figure caption. Four multicast trees are used to carry video traffic. For both schedulers, the maximum number of simultaneous retransmission requests is 2 per parent. Please note, however, that in both cases, retransmission requests are distortion-optimized.

The graphs indicate the average decoded video quality for the peers, for different playout deadlines. When the latency constraint is lax, both schedulers perform very closely for all the video sequences. For shorter playout deadlines, CoDiO P2P maintains higher performance than the sequential scheduler. For example, for an end-to-end latency constraint of 0.8 s, the gains for CoDiO P2P is between 1.0 and 2.0 dB for the different sequences, except *News* for which there is no significant difference. In other words, CoDiO P2P extends the limits of the system in terms of latency. The video quality drop-off for CoDiO P2P occurs for latencies lower by 15%, on average, and a latency reduction of up to 20% is achieved for the *Foreman* sequence. Note, that sequences with more instantaneous rate variation - namely *Foreman* and *Mother and Daughter*- and sequences for which the encoding rate is higher - e.g., *Salesman*, lead to higher performance improvement. This is due to the higher level of congestion which they generate on the network.

Results for the same experiment are presented in Fig. 5.13, for a network of 300 peers. As the multicast trees carrying the video traffic are longer in this case (6 hops, on average, compared to 4 hops for 75 peers), the average end-to-end delay between the video source and the different peers is higher. As a consequence, the video quality drop-off occurs for longer playout deadlines and reducing congestion is even more important, as late packet arrivals are more difficult to avoid. This leads to an increase in the overall performance improvement achieved by CoDiO P2P, particularly noticeable for *Salesman* and *Foreman* for which a latency reduction of up to 40% is observed.

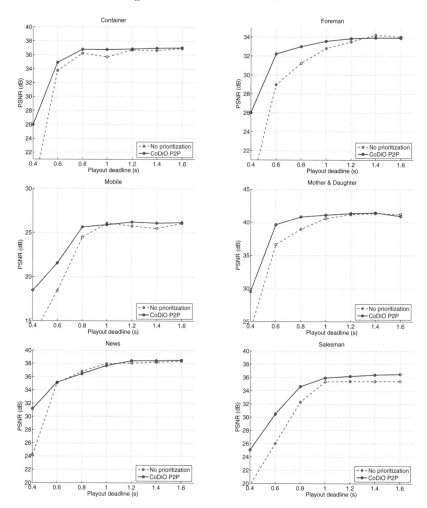

Fig. 5.12. Performance of CoDiO P2P compared to a non-prioritized sequential scheduler for 75 peers. Results shown for 6 sequences. The encoding rate for the sequences is as follows. Container: 283 kb/s, Foreman: 290 kb/s, Mobile: 342 kb/s, Mother & Daughter: 282 kb/s, News: 311 kb/s, Salesman: 364 kb/s.

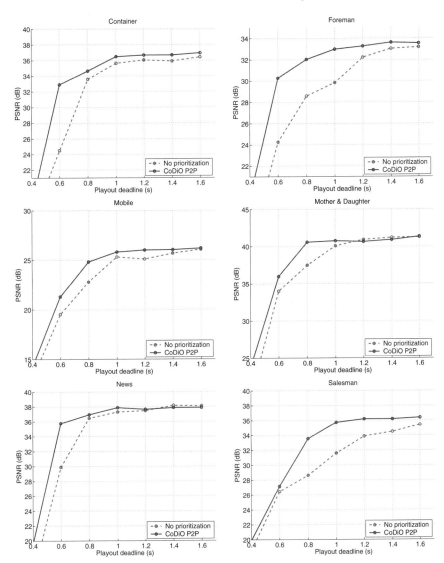

Fig. 5.13. Performance of CoDiO P2P compared to a non-prioritized sequential scheduler for 300 peers. Results shown for 6 sequences. The encoding rate for the sequences is as follows. Container: 283 kb/s, Foreman: 290 kb/s, Mobile: 342 kb/s, Mother & Daughter: 282 kb/s, News: 311 kb/s, Salesman: 364 kb/s.

5.4 Chapter Summary

In this chapter we describe an adaptive algorithm for streaming video from a single source to a large population of peers through the use of their forwarding capability. The different peers organize themselves in a distributed fashion in multiple multicast trees over which complementary portions of the video stream are transmitted. The system benefits from using more than one tree for distribution, as this leads to better use of the throughput of the peers. Most of the benefits of diversity is achieved by using two multicast trees in our simulation setup.

We study the performance of a congestion-distortion optimized video scheduler, CoDiO P2P, which combines two adaptive algorithms. The sender handles the prioritization of transmissions to its different descendants and favors, in particular, important video frames and peers forwarding video to large numbers of descendants. It spaces its transmissions to mitigate congestion created on its uplink. The receiver is a content-aware retransmission scheduler which is able to maintain video quality when a peer is partially disconnected from the network. This scheduler proceeds by requesting in priority packets which will lead to higher video distortion reduction. It distributes retransmission requests among its different parents with a limit on the additional burden created on their uplink. Compared to a simpler scheduler which does not use information on the content it is forwarding, CoDiO P2P improves the performance for low-latency streaming and achieves gains in terms of decoded video quality of up to 4 dB. It also maintains high video quality for playout deadlines which are 15-40% shorter. Our recent work [213], shows that CoDiO P2P also performs well compared to robust transport techniques which do not adapt to video content. In particular CoDiO P2P outperforms both multiple description coding and FEC for video streaming at high rates and with low latency.

6

Conclusions and Future Work

6.1 Conclusions

This book addresses the problem of video streaming with low latency over throughput-constrained networks and, in particular, over peer-to-peer (P2P) networks. The solutions we suggest span different parts of a video streaming system architecture, from the encoding, to the transport.

When throughput is limited, determining a suitable encoding rate is necessary to achieve sufficient video quality while avoiding self-inflicted congestion which may overwhelm the bottleneck of the network. Our rate-distortion model captures accurately the impact of rate on the end-to-end performance of the system and predicts the amount of over-provisioning needed to satisfy the constraints of low-latency streaming. To achieve very low latencies, we consider a congestion-distortion optimized scheduler which determines which packets to send, and when, to achieve high video quality while limiting self-congestion. Results indicate the benefits of using congestion to evaluate the performance of different schedules. Compared to rate-distortion optimization the scheduler reduces queuing delay as it shapes traffic to produce a network-friendly bitstream which minimizes large delay spikes on the bottleneck link.

Similar ideas can also be adapted to P2P video multicast where a video source transmits a stream synchronously to a large population of viewers by making use of the forwarding capacity of the connected peers. We study the advantages of congestion-distortion optimized packet scheduling for P2P networks and show how it can be performed, with very low complexity, by a scheme which combines an algorithm at the sender to prioritize transmissions destined to different peers and a retransmission scheduler at the receiver which sends distortion-optimized retransmission requests from a peer to its different forwarders. Experimental results for networks of several hundred peers show the benefit of adapting to the network topology and to the video content for low latencies.

6.2 Future Work

One of the contributions of this book is to illustrate the importance of considering congestion as a metric for media scheduling. It would be particularly well-suited to evaluate streaming systems which are based on wavelet video coding as they are usually designed for bandwidth-limited systems with varying throughput. Scheduling algorithms based on congestion and distortion should be investigated for these different types of media representations.

The SPPM P2P control protocol which we describe in Chapter 4 could be improved. An active tree management protocol which prevents low bandwidth peers from attaching to the highest parts of the tree would increase the throughput of the P2P network. Adjusting the frequency of hello message exchanges would reduce the total amount of control overhead. The join and rejoin latencies could be further reduced by changing the attachment process and not forcing peers to collect replies for all the probe packets they transmit. The results of recent deployments of SPPM at Stanford University will also help understand the limits of P2P video streaming, notably in terms of latency.

The growing popularity of video streaming over P2P networks makes it an exciting research topic particularly since adaptive video streaming in these environments is still in its early stages. Many good algorithms for server-client streaming systems can, and should, be adapted to P2P networks and will lead to interesting results. For example, adaptive media playout techniques would be a natural fit to these networks where end-to-end delay is likely to fluctuate and where reliability is difficult to guarantee. Efficient layered video coding schemes such as H.264 SVC would enable better adaptation to heterogeneous peers. Another possible direction is to study hybrid systems where a small set of servers is combined with a P2P network to alleviate the cost of the system in terms of infrastructure while providing quality of service guarantees, such as low startup delays or constant video quality. The scalability of these hybrid systems might even outperform that of P2P systems by providing more efficient and stable data distribution paths.

A

Video Experiments

We present in this appendix information pertaining to the video streaming experiments carried out in this work. We first present the video encoding structure chosen to compress sequences, then describe the latency-constrained video streaming process, and explain how we compute the peak-signal-to-noise-ratio (PSNR) which we use throughout the book as a video quality metric. Finally, we provide information on the 6 test sequences.

A.1 Video Streaming

A.1.1 Encoding Structures

The temporally layered scheme shown in Fig. A.1 is chosen to encode the video. For this open Group of Pictures (GOP), the first temporal layer is composed of I frames. The second temporal layer is composed of P frames. We restrict P frames to use as a reference the P frame or I frame preceding them in display order, as illustrated in the figure. The last layer is composed of B frames. We restrict the B frames to use as reference their two neighboring P frames or I frames[1]. This ensures good error resilience properties and allows to easily scale down the frame rate by 2 or even 4 if needed.

I B B B P B B B P B B B P B B B I

Fig. A.1. Encoding structure used for video streaming experiments with periodic I pictures. GOP length = 16

Table A.1 shows the other H.264 coding parameters chosen to generate the compressed sequences.

---

[1] Please note that these restrictions are not dictated by the H.264 standard.

Table A.1. H.264 encoding parameters

Hadamard transform	on
Search range	16 pixels
Number of reference frames	5
Hierarchical B frames	off
Entropy coding	CAVLC
Loop filter	on
Slices per picture	1
Rate-distortion optimization	on
Rate control	off

A.1.2 Latency-Constrained Video Streaming

In the video streaming experiments presented in this work, compressed video packets are made available at a sender, at a given time and need to be decoded shortly after at the receiver. Figure A.2, illustrates this process for the encoding structure shown in Fig. A.1.

As illustrated, the playout deadline is defined by the time between which the first frame of the sequence is made available at the sender and the time it is due at the decoder. Due to the dependencies between video frames, I frames and P frames are decoded 3 time slots before they are displayed. For the first frame of the sequence and for the B frames, the display and decoding times are identical.

A.1.3 Error-Resilient Decoding

We denote by $s(x, y, t)$ the luminance component of the original video signal, sampled on a regular grid of X by Y pixels, and by F the number of frames of the sequence. In the experiments we present, the video is compressed by an H.264 encoder and transmitted over a packet erasure channel. We denote by s_{dec} the decoded signal, recovered by the receiver.

Due to losses or to delay, all the data necessary to decode perfectly Frame t may not be available by the playout deadline of this frame. In this case, the decoder applies previous frame concealment:

$$s_{dec}(x, y, t) = s_{dec}(x, y, t - 1) \tag{A.1}$$

Previous frame concealment continues until a frame is received and decoded with no errors. This results in "freezing" Frame $t - 1$ over this time interval. The same process is also used to decode the color components of the video signal.

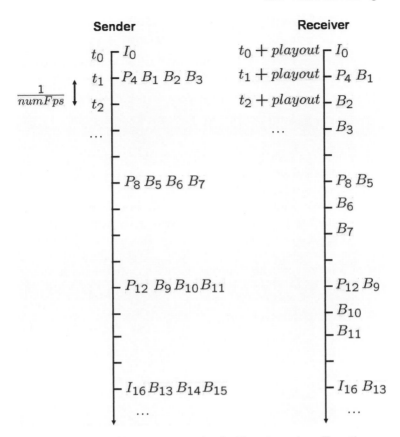

Fig. A.2. Illustration of latency-constrained video streaming. Two time axes are shown. The left axis shows the time at which frames are made available to the sender for transmission. The right axis shows when the different frames are due at the receiver. Frames are numbered, for clarity, in their display order. The first time slot at the sender and at the receiver is an exception, the rest of the process is periodic. The number of frames played by second is denoted by *numFps*. The playout deadline is denoted by *playout*.

A.1.4 Quality Metric

Throughout the book, we compute PSNR, as follows. First, the mean squared error of the luminance signal is computed, frame by frame:

$$MSE(t) = \frac{1}{XY} \sum_{x=1}^{X} \sum_{y=1}^{Y} (s(x, y, t) - s_{dec}(x, y, t))^2 \qquad (A.2)$$

For each frame, the PSNR can then be derived from the MSE:

$$PSNR(t) = 10 \log_{10} \frac{255^2}{MSE(t)} \qquad \text{(A.3)}$$

Finally, the average PSNR is computed by taking the average over all the frames of the sequence.

$$PSNR = \frac{1}{F} \sum_{t=1}^{F} PSNR(t) \qquad \text{(A.4)}$$

In the literature, the PSNR is sometimes computed *after*, computing the average of the MSE for all frames. In practice, however, there is no difference between these two definitions [214].

To ensure stable results, we loop the sequences at least 40 times and consider long channel traces, rather than repeating the experiments over multiple channel realizations[2]. This is motivated by the fact that the channels we consider are throughput-limited and have time-varying bottleneck queues. Considering long experiments is necessary to evaluate the performance of the system in steady state.

---

[2] The length of the simulations is indicated in the related sections of Chapters 3 and 5.

A.2 Video Sequences

Throughout this book, 6 standard test sequences are used to collect experimental results. In this section we provide additional information on the video sequences, focusing, in particular on their rate-distortion characteristics.

A.2.1 Container

Fig. A.3. Example picture of the sequence *Container*.

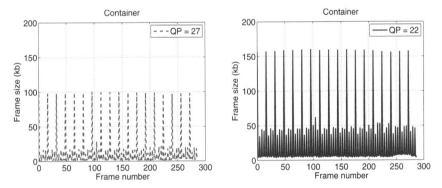

Fig. A.4. Left frame sizes for encoding rate 327 kb/s. Right: frame sizes for encoding rate 682 kb/s.

- **Sequence description:** video sequence captured with a fixed camera showing a container ship. The motion of the ship is slow and smooth. A small beating flag and a flight of birds, in the foreground, increase slightly the activity of the sequence.
- **Spatial resolution:** CIF, 288 x 352
- **Temporal resolution:** 30 frames per second
- **Number of frames:** 288 frames

Table A.2. Rate-distortion characteristics of the *Container* sequence, encoded with periodic I frames following the encoding structure shown in Fig. A.1.

QP	PSNR (dB)	Rate (kb/s)
20	41.92	896.64
21	41.25	782.61
22	40.64	681.92
23	39.87	581.98
24	39.22	502.59
25	38.71	442.45
26	37.87	372.62
27	37.24	327.01
28	36.62	283.42
29	35.97	244.13
30	35.38	214.72
31	34.85	191.19
32	34.19	164.65
33	33.66	145.02
34	33.04	128.30
35	32.40	112.16
36	31.83	98.18
37	31.32	88.68
38	30.61	77.39
39	30.08	69.80
40	29.52	62.07
41	28.91	55.34
42	28.31	49.29

A.2.2 Foreman

Fig. A.5. Example picture of the sequence *Foreman.*

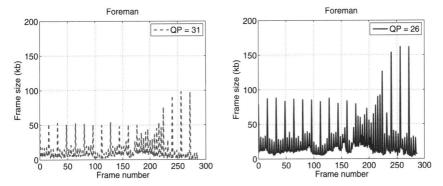

Fig. A.6. Left frame sizes for encoding rate 339 kb/s. Right: frame sizes for encoding rate 677 kb/s.

- **Sequence description:** sequence captured with a hand-held device, showing a talking head and a construction site. Motion is due to changes in facial expression and to camera motion which includes panning.
- **Spatial resolution:** CIF, 288 x 352
- **Temporal resolution:** 30 frames per second
- **Number of frames:** 288 frames

Table A.3. Rate-distortion characteristics of the *Foreman* sequence, encoded with periodic I frames following the encoding structure shown in Fig. A.1.

QP	PSNR (dB)	Rate (kb/s)
20	41.82	1739.98
21	41.15	1507.27
22	40.51	1293.22
23	39.78	1098.14
24	39.12	933.65
25	38.58	814.04
26	37.80	676.52
27	37.18	586.97
28	36.57	502.58
29	35.92	435.35
30	35.31	380.01
31	34.76	338.99
32	34.08	290.11
33	33.54	256.76
34	32.92	227.37
35	32.30	198.99
36	31.71	175.43
37	31.19	160.11
38	30.53	139.37
39	29.99	125.67
40	29.42	113.28
41	28.75	101.31
42	28.22	90.99

A.2.3 Mobile

Fig. A.7. Example picture of the sequence *Mobile*.

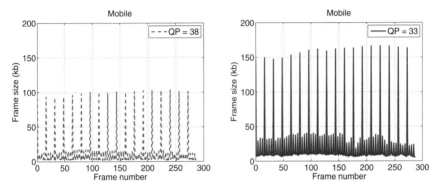

Fig. A.8. Left frame sizes for encoding rate 339 kb/s. Right: frame sizes for encoding rate 677 kb/s.

- **Sequence description:** active sequence with camera zoom and pan. Moving objects in the foreground and camera motion cause the background to be covered and uncovered.
- **Spatial resolution:** CIF, 288 x 352
- **Temporal resolution:** 30 frames per second
- **Number of frames:** 288 frames

Table A.4. Rate-distortion characteristics of the *Mobile* sequence, encoded with periodic I frames following the encoding structure shown in Fig. A.1.

QP	PSNR (dB)	Rate (kb/s)
20	40.83	4517.24
21	39.98	4045.62
22	39.16	3612.61
23	38.22	3146.58
24	37.32	2746.84
25	36.60	2442.04
26	35.58	2055.70
27	34.76	1783.24
28	33.93	1518.26
29	33.03	1271.54
30	32.23	1098.17
31	31.56	955.70
32	30.71	799.03
33	30.04	686.19
34	29.31	600.18
35	28.56	511.31
36	27.88	443.47
37	27.30	400.08
38	26.55	342.11
39	25.92	305.98
40	25.28	267.12
41	24.57	237.07
42	23.94	207.83

A.2.4 Mother & Daughter

Fig. A.9. Example picture of the sequence *Mother & Daughter.*

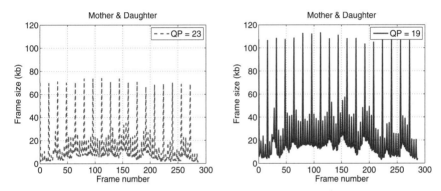

Fig. A.10. Left frame sizes for encoding rate 368 kb/s. Right: frame sizes for encoding rate 687 kb/s.

- **Sequence description:** video conference sequence captured with a fixed camera. There are two people in the foreground, one of which is talking, and a fixed background. The sequence displays limited motion mostly due to changes in facial expression and to arm motion of one of the characters.
- **Spatial resolution:** CIF, 288 x 352
- **Temporal resolution:** 30 frames per second
- **Number of frames:** 288 frames

Table A.5. Rate-distortion characteristics of the *Mother & Daughter* sequence, encoded with periodic I frames following the encoding structure shown in Fig. A.1.

QP	PSNR (dB)	Rate (kb/s)
19	44.48	686.54
20	43.94	566.96
21	43.42	493.74
22	42.89	426.66
23	42.28	367.70
24	41.74	318.67
25	41.29	281.55
26	40.54	239.32
27	39.97	211.81
28	39.37	184.62
29	38.76	161.18
30	38.12	142.32
31	37.57	126.80
32	36.92	109.50
33	36.38	97.08
34	35.75	85.61
35	35.09	75.52
36	34.58	65.85
37	34.13	59.38
38	33.44	51.22
39	33.09	45.61
40	32.48	40.13
41	31.88	35.32
42	31.36	31.37

A.2.5 News

Fig. A.11. Example picture of the sequence *News*.

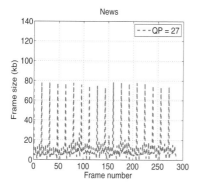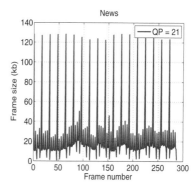

Fig. A.12. Left frame sizes for encoding rate 356 kb/s. Right: frame sizes for encoding rate 702 kb/s.

- **Sequence description:** typical news sequence, captured with a fixed camera, featuring an anchorman and an anchorwoman whose facial expression change moderately. Most of the activity of the sequence is caused by a large screen displaying an excerpt of a ballet with camera pan, in the background. The screen fills approximately one fifth of the picture.
- **Spatial resolution:** CIF, 288 x 352
- **Temporal resolution:** 30 frames per second
- **Number of frames:** 288 frames

Table A.6. Rate-distortion characteristics of the *News* sequence, encoded with periodic I frames following the encoding structure shown in Fig. A.1.

QP	PSNR (dB)	Rate (kb/s)
20	43.71	781.75
21	43.14	701.54
22	42.56	629.96
23	41.88	558.17
24	41.27	499.11
25	40.76	453.21
26	39.99	396.06
27	39.36	357.87
28	38.70	319.14
29	37.98	282.57
30	37.32	255.58
31	36.72	231.66
32	35.96	203.80
33	35.36	182.84
34	34.69	164.98
35	33.96	145.40
36	33.27	129.36
37	32.68	118.51
38	31.88	103.48
39	31.29	94.22
40	30.61	83.59
41	29.88	74.78
42	29.27	66.93

A.2.6 Salesman

Fig. A.13. Example picture of the sequence *Salesman*.

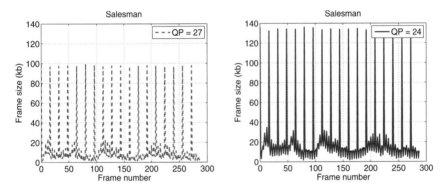

Fig. A.14. Left frame sizes for encoding rate 364 kb/s. Right: frame sizes for encoding rate 627 kb/s.

- **Description:** sequence captured with a fixed camera. The only motion is due to the limited motion of the character in the foreground. The background is fixed.
- **Spatial resolution:** CIF, 288 x 352
- **Temporal resolution:** 30 frames per second
- **Number of frames:** 288 frames

Table A.7. Rate-distortion characteristics of the *Salesman* sequence, encoded with periodic I frames following the encoding structure shown in Fig. A.1.

QP	PSNR (dB)	Rate (kb/s)
20	41.25	1452.18
21	40.54	1176.61
22	39.90	967.55
23	39.18	770.83
24	38.58	626.91
25	38.06	524.45
26	37.38	427.17
27	36.79	364.28
28	36.23	311.00
29	35.63	265.20
30	35.06	233.44
31	34.53	207.62
32	33.87	178.64
33	33.35	158.38
34	32.72	139.84
35	32.07	121.71
36	31.48	106.83
37	30.99	97.23
38	30.29	84.23
39	29.76	75.59
40	29.14	66.22
41	28.52	57.71
42	27.96	50.64

References

1. "Peer-to-peer in 2005," *Online report, available at http://www.cachelogic.com/research/2005_slide07.php, seen on Apr. 2nd 2006.*
2. *Advanced Video Coding for Generic Audiovisual services, ITU-T Recommendation H.264 - ISO/IEC 14496-10(AVC),* ITU-T and ISO/IEC JTC 1, 2003.
3. *ITU-T, Video Codec for Audiovisual Services at px64 kbit/s, ITU-T Recommendation H.261, Version 1: Nov. 1990; Version 2: Mar. 1993.*
4. *ISO/IEC JTC 1, "Coding of moving pictures and associated audio for digital storage media at up to about 1.5 Mbit/s Part 2: Video," ISO/IEC 11172-2 (MPEG-1), Mar. 1993.*
5. *ITU-T and ISO/IEC JTC 1, Generic coding of moving pictures and associated audio information Part 2: Video, ITU-T Recommendation H.262 ISO/IEC 13818-2 (MPEG-2), Nov. 1994.*
6. *ITU-T, Video coding for low bit rate communication, ITUT Recommendation H.263; version 1, Nov. 1995; version 2, Jan. 1998; version 3, Nov. 2000.*
7. *ISO/IEC JTC1, Coding of audio-visual objects Part 2: Visual, ISO/IEC 14496-2 (MPEG-4 visual version 1), April 1999; Amendment 1 (version 2), February, 2000; Amendment 4 (streaming profile), January, 2001.*
8. Y. Wang, J. Ostermann, and Y.-Q. Zhang, *Video Processing and Communications.* Prentice Hall, New Jersey, 2001.
9. A. Luthra, G. Sullivan, and T. Wiegand (Eds.), "Special Issue on the H.264/AVC Video Coding Standard," *IEEE Circuits and Systems Magazine,* vol. 13, no. 7, Jul. 2003.
10. J. Ostermann, J. Bormans, P. List, D. Marpe, M. Narroschke, F. Pereira, T. Stockhammer, and T. Wedi, "Video Coding with H.264/AVC: Tools, Performance, and Complexity," *IEEE Circuits and Systems Magazine,* vol. 4, no. 1, pp. 7–28, Jan. 2004.
11. B. Erol, A. Dumitras, F. Kossentini, A. Joch, and G. Sullivan, *MPEG-4, H.264/AVC, and MPEG-7: New Standards for the Digital Video Industry, in Handbook of image and video processing, 2nd Ed.* Academic Press, 2005.
12. S. Srinivasan, P. Hsu, T. Holcomb, K. Mukerjee, S. Regunathan, B. Lin, J. Liang, M.-C. Lee, and J. Ribas-Corbera, "Windows Media Video 9: Overview and Applications," *Signal Processing: Image Communications,* vol. 19, no. 9, pp. 851–875, Oct. 2004.

13. G. Srinivasan and S. Regunathan, "An overvriew of VC-1," *Proc. of SPIE, Visual Communications and Image Processing, Beijing, China*, vol. 5960, pp. 720–728, Jul. 2005.

14. L. Yu, F. Yi, J. Dong, and C. Zhang, "Overview of AVS-video: Tools, Performance and Complexity," *Proc. of SPIE, Visual Communications and Image Processing, Beijing, China*, vol. 5960, pp. 679–689, Jul. 2005.

15. T. Wedi and H. Musmann, "Motion- and Aliasing-Compensated Prediction for Hybrid Video Coding," *IEEE Transactions on Circuits and Systems for Video Technology*, vol. 13, no. 7, pp. 577–586, Jul. 2003.

16. D. Marpe, H. Schwarz, and T. Wiegand, "Context-Adaptive Binary Arithmetic Coding in the H.264/AVC Video Compression Standard," *IEEE Transactions on Circuits and Systems for Video Technology*, vol. 13, no. 7, pp. 620–636, Jul. 2003.

17. "H.264/AVC Reference Software," *http://iphome.hhi.de/suehring/tml/download/, seen on Aug. 28 2005*.

18. G. Sullivan and T. Wiegand, "Video Compression - From Concepts to the H.264/AVC Standard," *Proc. of the IEEE, Special Issue on Advances in Video Coding and Delivery*, vol. 93, no. 1, pp. 18–31, Jan. 2005.

19. G. Sullivan, P. Topiwala, and A. Luthra, "The H.264/AVC Advanced Video Coding Standard: Overview and Introduction to the Fidelity Range Extensions," *SPIE Annual Conference on Applications of Digital Image Processing XXVII, Special Session on Advances in the New Emerging Standard H.264/AVC*, pp. 454–474, Aug. 2004.

20. H. Schwarz, D. Marpe, and T. Wiegand, "MCTF and Scalability Extension of H.264/AVC," *Proc. Picture Coding Symposium (PCS 2004), San Francisco, CA, USA*, Dec. 2004.

21. ——, "SNR-Scalable Extension of H.264/AVC," *Proc. IEEE Int. Conference on Image Processing (ICIP), Singapore*, Oct. 2004.

22. B. Girod, "The Efficiency of Motion-Compensating Prediction for Hybrid Coding of Video Sequences," *IEEE Journal on Selected Areas in Communications*, vol. 5, no. 7, pp. 1140–1154, Aug. 1987.

23. ——, "Motion-Compensating Prediction with Fractional Pel Accuracy," *IEEE Transactions on Communications*, vol. 41, pp. 604–612, Apr. 1993.

24. ——, "Efficiency Analysis of Multi-Hypothesis Motion-Compensated Prediction for Video Coding," *IEEE Trans. Image Processing*, vol. 9, no. 2, pp. 173–183, Feb. 2000.

25. M. Flierl and B. Girod, "Multihypothesis Motion Estimation for Video Coding," *Proc. of the Data Compression Conference, Snowbird, USA*, Mar. 2001.

26. ——, "Multihypothesis Motion-Compensated Prediction with Forward Adaptive Hypothesis Switching," *Proc. Picture Coding Symposium, Seoul, Korea*, Apr. 2001.

27. M. H. Flierl, *Video Coding with Superimposed Motion-Compensated Signals, Ph.D. Dissertation, University of Erlangen*, 2003.

28. G. Cook, J. Prades-Nebot, and E. Delp, "Rate-Distortion Bounds for Motion-Compensated Rate Scalable Video Coders," *Proc. Int. Conference on Image Processing (ICIP), Singapore*, pp. 3121–3124, Oct. 2004.

29. J. Prades-Nebot, G. Cook, and E. Delp, "Analysis of the Efficiency of SNR-Scalable Strategies for Motion Compensated Video Coders," *Proc. Int. Conference on Image Processing (ICIP), Singapore*, pp. 3109–3112, Oct. 2004.

30. Z. He and S. Mitra, "A Unified Rate-Distortion Analysis Framework for Transform Coding," *IEEE Transactions on Circuits and Systems for Video Technology*, vol. 11, no. 12, pp. 1221–1236, dec 2001.

31. K. Stuhlmüller, N. Färber, M. Link, and B. Girod, "Analysis of Video Transmission over Lossy Channels," *IEEE Journal on Selected Areas in Communications*, vol. 18, no. 6, pp. 1012–32, June 2000.

32. R. Zhang, S. Regunathan, and K. Rose, "End-to-end Distortion Estimation for RD-based Robust Delivery of Pre-compressed Video," *Thirty-Fifth Asilomar Conference on Signals, Systems and Computers, Pacific Grove, USA*, Nov. 2001.

33. G. Cote, S. Shirani, and F. Kossentini, "Optimal Mode Selection And Synchronization For Robust Video Communication Over Error-Prone Networks," *IEEE Journal on Selected Areas in Communications*, vol. 18, no. 6, pp. 952–956, Jun. 2000.

34. Y. Eisenberg, F. Zhai, C. Luna, T. Pappas, R. Berry, and A. Katsaggelos, "Variance-Aware Distortion Estimation for Wireless Video Communications," *Proc. Int. Conference on Image Processing (ICIP), Barcelona, Spain*, vol. 1, pp. 89–92, Sep. 2003.

35. Y. Liang, J. Apostolopoulos, and B. Girod, "Analysis of Packet Loss for Compressed Video: Does Burst-Length Matter?" *Proc. IEEE Int. Conference on Acoustics, Speech, and Signal Processing (ICASSP), Hong Kong, China*.

36. J. Chakareski, J. Apostolopoulos, W. t. Tan, S. Wee, and B. Girod, "Distortion Chains for Predicting for Video Distortion for General Loss Patterns," *Proc. IEEE Int. Conference on Acoustics, Speech, and Signal Processing (ICASSP), Montreal, Canada*, May 2004.

37. W. Zhu, M.-T. Sun, L.-G. Chen, and T. Sikora (Eds.), "Special Issue on Advances in Video Coding and Delivery," *Proc. of the IEEE*, vol. 93, no. 1, Jan. 2005.

38. W. Zeng, K. Nahrstedt, P. Chou, A. Ortega, P. Frossard, and H. Yu (Eds.), "Special issue on streaming media," *IEEE Transactions on Multimedia*, vol. 6, no. 2, Apr. 2004.

39. B. Girod, M. Kalman, Y. Liang, and R. Zhang, "Advances in Channel-adaptive Video Streaming," *Wireless Communications and Mobile Computing*, vol. 6, no. 2, pp. 549–552, Sep. 2002.

40. M. Civanlar, A. Luthra, S. Wenger, and W. Zhu (Eds.), "Special Issue on Streaming Video," *IEEE Transactions on Circuits and Systems for Video Technology*, vol. 11, no. 3, Mar. 2001.

41. J. Apostolopoulos and M. Conti (Eds.), "Special Issue on Multimedia over Broadband Wireless Networks," *IEEE Networks*, vol. 20, no. 2, pp. 1721–1737, Mar. 2006.

42. B. Girod, I. Lagenduk, Q. Zhang, and W. Zhu (Eds.), "Special Issue on Advances in Wireless Video," *IEEE Wireless Communications*, vol. 12, no. 4, Aug. 2005.

43. R. Chandramouli, R. Shorey, P. Srimani, X. Wang, and H. Yu (Eds.), "Special Issue on Recent Advances in Wireless Multimedia," *Journal on Selected Areas in Communications*, vol. 21, no. 10, pp. 1721–1737, Dec. 2003.

44. Y. Wang and Q.-F. Zhu, "Error Control and Concealment for Video Communication: a Review," *Proc. of the IEEE*, vol. 86, no. 5, pp. 974–997, May 1998.

45. Y. Wang, S. Wenger, J. Wen, and A. Katsaggelos, "Error Resilient Video Coding Techniques," *IEEE Signal Processing Magazine*, vol. 17, no. 4, pp. 61–82, Jul. 2000.

46. B. Girod and N. Färber, *Wireless Video, in A. Reibman, M.-T. Sun (Eds.), Compressed Video over Networks,*. Marcel Dekker, 1999.

47. S. Wenger, "H.264/AVC over IP," *IEEE Transactions on Circuits and Systems for Video Technology*, vol. 13, no. 7, pp. 645–656, Jul. 2003.

48. S. Blake, D. Black, M. Carlson, E. Davies, Z. Wang, and W. Weiss, "An Architecture for Differentiated Services," *IETF RFC 2475*, Dec. 1998.

49. R. Braden, L. Zhang, S. Berson, S. Herzog, and S. Jamin, "Resource ReSerVation Protocol (RSVP)," *IETF RFC 2205*, Sep. 1997.

50. G. Cote and F. Kossentini, "Optimal Intra Coding of Blocks for Robust Communication over the Internet," *Signal Processing: Image Communication*, vol. 15, no. 1-2, pp. 25–34, Sep. 1999.

51. R. Zhang, S. Regunathan, and K. Rose, "Video Coding with Optimal Inter/Intra-Mode Switching for Packet Loss Resilience," *IEEE Journal on Selected Areas in Communications*, vol. 18, no. 6, pp. 966–976, Jun. 2000.

52. T. Stockhammer, M. Hannuksela, and T. Wiegand, "H.264/AVC in Wireless Environments," *IEEE Transactions on Circuits and Systems*, vol. 13, no. 7, pp. 657–673, Jul. 2003.

53. S. Lin, S. Mao, and Y. Wang, "A Reference Picture Selection Scheme for Video Transmission over Ad Hoc Networks using Multiple Paths," *Proc. IEEE Int. Conference on Multimedia and Expo (ICME), Tokyo, Japan*, Aug. 2001.

54. Y. J. Liang, M. Flierl, and B. Girod, "Low Latency Video Transmission over Lossy Packet Networks using Rate-Distortion Optimized Reference Picture Selection," *Proc. Int. Conference on Image Processing (ICIP), Rochester, USA*, pp. 181–184, Sep. 2002.

55. Y. Liang, E. Setton, and B. Girod, "Network-Adaptive Video Communication Using Packet Path Diversity and Rate-Distortion Optimized Reference Picture Selection," *Journal of VLSI Signal Processing Systems for Signal, Image, and Video Technology*, vol. 41, no. 3, Nov. 2005.

56. W. Tu and E. Steinbach, "Proxy-Based Reference Picture Selection for Real-Time Video Transmission Over Mobile Networks," *Proc. IEEE Int. Conference on Multimedia and Expo (ICME), Amsterdam, The Netherlands*, pp. 309–312, Jul. 2005.

57. E. Setton, Y. Liang, and B. Girod, "Adaptive Multiple Description Video Streaming over Multiple Channels with Active Probing," *Proc. IEEE Int. Conference on Multimedia and Expo (ICME), Baltimore, USA*, vol. 1, pp. 509–512, Jul. 2003.

58. Y. Liang and B. Girod, "Low-latency Streaming of Pre-Encoded Video Using Channel-Adaptive Bitstream Assembly," *Proc. IEEE Int. Conference on Multimedia and Expo (ICME), Lausanne, Switzerland*, pp. 873–876, Jul. 2002.

59. E. Setton, A. Shionozaki, and B. Girod, "Real-time Streaming of Prestored Multiple Description Video with Restart," *Proc. IEEE Int. Conference on Multimedia and Expo (ICME), Taipe, Taiwan*, vol. 2, pp. 1323–1326, jul 2004.

60. H.-K. Cheung, Y.-L. Chan, and W.-C. Siu, "Reference Picture Selection in an Already MPEG Encoded Bitstream," *Proc. IEEE Int. Conference on Image Processing (ICIP), Genoa, Italy*, vol. 1, pp. 793–796, Sep. 2005.

61. A. Albanese, J. Blömer, J. Edmonds, M. Luby, and M. Sudan, "Priority Encoding Transmission," *IEEE Trans. Information Theory*, vol. 42, pp. 1737–1744, Nov. 1996.

62. U. Horn, K. Stuhlmüller, M. Link, and B. Girod, "Robust Internet Video Transmission Based on Scalable Coding and Unequal Error Protection," *Signal Processing: Image Communication*, vol. 15, no. 1-2, pp. 77–94, Sep. 1999.

63. A. Mohr, E. Riskin, and R. Ladner, "Unequal Loss Protection: Graceful Degradation of Image Quality over Packet Erasure Channels through Forward Error Correction," *IEEE Journal on Selected Areas in Communications*, vol. 18, no. 6, pp. 819–829, Jun. 2000.

64. W. Zhu, Q. Zhang, and Y.-Q. Zhang, "Network-Adaptive Rate Control with Unequal Loss Protection for Scalable Video over Internet," *Proc. Int. Symp. Circuits and Systems, Sydney, Australia*, May 2001.

65. R. Puri and K. Ramchandran, "Multiple Description Source Coding through Forward Error Correction Codes," *Proc. IEEE Asilomar Conf. Signals, Systems, and Computers, Asilomar, USA*, vol. 1, pp. 342–246, Oct. 1999.

66. D. Turner and K. Ross, "Optimal Streaming of Layered-Encoded Multimedia Presentations," *Proc. IEEE Int. Conf. on Multimedia and Expo (ICME), New York, USA*, Jul. 2000.

67. T. Tian, A. Li, J. Wen, and J. Villasenor, "Prority Dropping in Network Transmission of Scalable Video," *Proc. IEEE Int. Conf. on Image Processing (ICIP), Vancouver, Canada*, vol. 3, pp. 400–403, Oct. 2000.

68. S. Dumitrescu, Z. Wang, and X. Wu, "Globally Optimal Uneven Error-Protected Packetization of Scalable Code Streams," *Proc. of the Data Compression Conference, Snowbird, USA*, pp. 73–82, Sep. 2002.

69. J. Boyce, "Packet Loss Resilient Transmission of MPEG Video over the Internet," *Signal Processing: Image Communication*, vol. 15, no. 1-2, pp. 7–24, Sep. 1999.

70. M. Hannuksela, Y.-K. Wang, and M. Gabbouj, "Isolated Regions in Video Coding," *IEEE Trans. on Multimedia*, vol. 6, no. 2, pp. 259–267, Apr. 2004.

71. P. Baccichet, S. Rane, A. Chimienti, and B. Girod, "Robust Low-Delay Video Transmission using H.264/AVC Redundant Slices and Flexible Macroblock Ordering," *Proc. IEEE Int. Conference on Image Processing (ICIP), to appear*, Oct. 2007.

72. S. Wicker, *Error Control Systems for Digital Communication and Storage*. Prentice Hall, 1995.

73. B. Dempsey, J. Liebeherr, and A. Weaver, "On Retransmission-Based Error Control for Continuous Media Traffic in Packet-Switching Networks," *Computer Networks and ISDN Systems Journal*, vol. 28, no. 5, pp. 719–736, Mar. 1996.

74. C. Papadopoulos and G. Parulkar, "Retransmission-Based Error Control for Continuous Media Applications," *Proceedings of the Sixth International Workshop on Network and Operating System Support for Digital Audio and Video (NOSSDAV), Zushi, Japan*, pp. 5–12, Jul. 1996.

75. M. Podolsky, S. McCanne, and M. Vetterli, "Soft ARQ for Layered Streaming Media," *Tech. Rep. UCB/CSD-98-1024, University of California, Computer Science Division, Berkeley*, Nov. 1998.

76. Z. Miao and A. Ortega, "Optimal Scheduling for Streaming of Scalable Media," *Proc. IEEE Asilomar Conf. Signals, Systems, and Computers, Pacific Grove, USA*, vol. 2, pp. 1357–1362, Nov. 2000.

77. P. Chou and Z. Miao, "Rate-Distortion Optimized Streaming of Packetized Media," *Microsoft Research Technical Report MSR-TR-2001-35*, Feb. 2001.

78. ——, "Rate-Distortion Optimized Streaming of Packetized Media," *IEEE Transactions on Multimedia*, vol. 8, no. 2, pp. 390–404, Apr. 2006.

79. M. Kalman, P. Ramanathan, and B. Girod, "Rate-Distortion Optimized Streaming with Multiple Deadlines," *Proc. Int. Conference on Image Processing (ICIP), Barcelona, Spain*, vol. 5, pp. 3145–3148, Sep. 2003.

80. J. Chakareski, P. Chou, and B. Girod, "Rate-Distortion Optimized Streaming from the Edge of the Network," *Proc. IEEE Fifth Workshop on Multimedia Signal Processing (MMSP), St. Thomas, Virgin Islands*, Dec. 2002.

81. J. Chakareski and B. Girod, "Rate-distortion Optimized Media Streaming with Rich Requests," *Proc. Packet Video Workshop, Irvine, USA*, Dec. 2004.

82. M. Röder, J. Cardinal, and R. Hamzaoui, "On the Complexity of Rate-Distortion Optimal Streaming of Packetized Media," *Proc. Data Compression Conference, Snowbird, USA*, Mar. 2004.

83. S. Wee, W. Tan, J. Apostolopoulos, and M. Etoh, "Optimized Video Streaming for Networks with Varying Delay," *Proc. IEEE Int. Conference on Multimedia and Expo (ICME), Lausanne, Switzerland*, Aug. 2002.

84. J. Chakareski, J. Apostolopoulos, S. Wee, W. Tan, and B. Girod, "Rate-Distortion Hint Tracks for Adaptive Video Streaming," *IEEE Transactions on Circuits and Systems for Video Technology*, vol. 15, no. 10, pp. 1257–1269, Oct. 2005.

85. M. Kalman and B. Girod, "Rate-Distortion Optimized Video Streaming with Multiple Deadlines for Low Latency Applications," *Proc. Packet Video Workshop, Irvine, USA*, Dec. 2004.

86. ——, "Rate-distortion Optimized Video Streaming Using Conditional Packet Delay Distributions," *Proc. IEEE Int. Workshop on Multimedia Signal Processing (MMSP), Siena, Italy*, Sep. 2004.

87. J. Chakareski and B. Girod, "Rate-Distortion Optimized Packet Scheduling and Routing for Media Streaming with Path Diversity," *Proc. IEEE Data Compression Conference, Snowbird, USA*, Apr. 2003.

88. R. Thoma and M. Bierling, "Motion Compensated Interpolation Considering Covered and Uncovered Background," *Signal Processing: Image Communication*, vol. 1, no. 2, pp. 192–212, Oct. 1989.

89. J. K. Su and R. Mersereau, "Motion-Compensated Interpolation of Untransmitted Frames in Compressed Video," *Proc. 30th Asilomar Conf. on Signals Systems and Computers, Asilomar, USA*, pp. 100–104, Nov. 1996.

90. P. Csillag and L. Boroczky, "Enhancement of Video Data using Motion-Compensated Postprocessing Techniques," *Proc. Int. Conference on Acoustics, Speech, and Signal Processing, Munich, Germany*, vol. 4, pp. 2897–2900, Apr. 1997.

91. E. Quacchio, E. Magli, G. Olmo, P. Baccichet, and A. Chimienti, "Enhancing Whole-Frame Error Concealment with an Intra Motion Vector Estimator in H.264/AVC," *Proc. Int. Conference on Acoustics, Speech, and Signal Processing, Philadelphia, USA*, pp. 329–332, Mar. 2005.

92. G. Conklin, G. Greenbaum, K. Lillevold, A. Lippman, and Y. Reznik, "Video Coding for Streaming Media Delivery on the Internet," *IEEE Transactions on Circuits and Systems for Video Technology*, vol. 11, no. 3, pp. 269–281, Mar. 2001.

93. M. Allman, V. Paxson, and W. R. Stevens, "TCP Congestion Control," *RFC 2581*, Apr. 1999.

94. M. Handley, S. Floyd, J. Pahdye, and J. Widmer, "TCP Friendly Rate Control (TFRC): Protocol Specification," *RFC 3448*, Jan. 2003.

95. D. Bansal and H. Balakrishnan, "Binomial Congestion Control," *Proc. IEEE INFOCOM, Anchorage, USA*, Apr. 2001.

96. H. Balakrishnan and R. Katz, "Explicit Loss Notification and Wireless Web Performance," *Proc. Globecom, Sydney, Australia*, Nov. 1998.

97. M. Sharma, D. Katabi, R. Pan, and B. Prabhakar, "A General Multiplexed ECN Channel and its use for Wireless Loss Notification," *Proc. ACM SIG-COMM, Karlsruhe, Germany*, Aug. 2003.

98. A. Markopoulou, E. Setton, M. Kalman, and J. Apostolopoulos, "Wise Video: Improving Rate-controlled Video Streaming Using in-band Wireless Loss Notification," *Proc. IEEE Int. Conference on Multimedia and Expo (ICME), Taipei, Taiwan*, Jul. 2004.

99. M. Chen and A. Zakhor, "Rate Control for Streaming Video over Wireless," *Proc. Infocom, Hong-Kong, China*, Mar. 2004.

100. H. Kanakia, P. Mishra, and A. Reibman, "An Adaptive Congestion Control Scheme for Real Time Packet Video Transport," *IEEE/ACM Transactions on Networking*, vol. 3, no. 6, pp. 671–682, Dec. 1995.

101. J. Webb and K. Oehler, "A Simple Rate-Distortion Model, Parameter Estimation, and Application to Real-Time Rate Control for DCT-Based Coders," *Proc. Int. Conference on Image Processing (ICIP), Santa Barbara, USA*, vol. 2, pp. 13–16, oct 1997.

102. K. H. Yang, A. Jacquin, and N. Jayant, "A Normalized Rate-Distortion Model for H.263-Compatible Codecs and its Application to Quantizer Selection," *Proc. Int. Conference on Image Processing, Santa Barbara, USA*, vol. 2, pp. 41–44, oct 1997.

103. L.-J. Lin and A. Ortega, "Bit-Rate Control using Piecewise Approximated Rate-Distortion Characteristics," *IEEE Transactions on Circuits and Systems for Video Technology*, vol. 8, no. 4, pp. 446–459, aug 1998.

104. J. Ribas-Corbera and S. Lei, "Rate Control in DCT Video Coding for Low-Delay Communications," *IEEE Transactions on Circuits and Systems for Video Technology*, vol. 9, no. 1, pp. 172–185, feb 1999.

105. Z. Li, F. Pan, K. Lim, X. Lin, and S. Rahardja, "Adaptive Rate Control for H.264," *Proc. IEEE Int. Conference on Image Processing (IEEE), Singapore*, pp. 745–748, Oct. 2004.

106. K. Lee, R. Puri, T. Kim, K. Ramchandran, and V. Bharghavan, "An Integrated Source Coding and Congestion Control Framework for Video Streaming in the Internet," *Proc. of the IEEE INFOCOM, Tel Aviv, Israel*, Mar. 2000.

107. N. Feamster, D. Bansal, and H. Balakrishnan, "On the Interactions Between Layered Quality Adaptation and Congestion Control for Video Streaming," *Proc. 11th Int. Packet Video Workshop, Kyongju, Korea*, May 2001.

108. T. Schierl and T. Wiegand, "H.264/AVC Rate Adaption for Internet Streaming," *Proc. Int. Packet Video Workshop, Irvine, USA*, Dec. 2004.

109. T. Nguyen and J. Ostermann, "Streaming and Congestion Control using Scalable Video Coding Based on H.264/AVC," *Proc. 15th Int. Packet Video Workshop, Hangzhou, China*, pp. 749–754, Apr. 2006.

110. I. Ahmad, X. Wei, Y. Sun, and Y.-Q. Zhang, "Video Transcoding: an Overview of Various Techniques and Research Issues," *IEEE Transactions on Multimedia*, vol. 7, no. 5, pp. 793–804, Oct. 2005.

111. W. Tan and G. Cheung, "SP-Frame Selection for Video Streaming over Burst-loss Networks," *Proc. IEEE Int. Symposium on Multimedia, Irvine, USA*, Dec. 2005.

112. J. Chakareski and B. Girod, "Rate-Distortion Optimized Video Streaming Over Internet Packet Traces," *Proc. IEEE Int. Conference on Image Processing (ICIP), Genoa, Italy*, vol. 2, pp. 161–164, Sep. 2005.

113. T. Stockhammer, M. Walter, and G. Liebl, "Optimized H. 264-Based Bit-stream Switching for Wireless Video Streaming," *Proc. IEEE Int. Conference on Multimedia and Expo, Amsterdam, Netherlands*, pp. 1396–1399, Jul. 2005.

114. D. Andersen, H. Balakrishnan, M. Kaashoek, and R. Morris, "The Case for Resilient Overlay Networks," *Proc. of the 8th Annual Workshop on Hot Topics in Operating Systems, Elmau, Germany*, May 2001.

115. J. G. Apostolopoulos, "Reliable Video Communication over Lossy Packet Networks using Multiple State Encoding and Path Diversity," *Proc. of SPIE Conference on Visual Communicatins and Image Processing (VCIP), San Jose, USA*, pp. 392–409, Jan. 2001.

116. V. Goyal, "Multiple Description Coding: Compression Meets the Network," *IEEE Signal Processing Magazine*, vol. 18, no. 5, pp. 74–93, Sep. 2001.

117. Y. Wang, S. Panwar, S. Lin, and S. Mao, "Wireless Video Transport using Path Diversity: Multiple Description vs. Layered Coding," *Proc. IEEE Int. Conference on Image Processing (ICIP), Rochester, USA*, pp. 21–24, Sep. 2002.

118. A. Majumdar, R. Puri, and K. Ramchandran, "Distributed Multimedia Transmission from Multiple Servers," *Proc. IEEE Int. Conference on Image Processing (ICIP), Rochester, USA*, pp. 177–180, Sep. 2002.

119. S. Mao, S. Lin, S. Panwar, Y. Wang, and E. Celebi, "Video Transport over Ad Hoc Networks: Multistream Coding with Multipath Transport," *IEEE Journal on Selected Areas in Communications*, vol. 21, no. 10, pp. 1721–1737, Dec. 2003.

120. A. Begen, Y. Altunbasak, O. Ergun, and M. Ammar, "Multipath Selection for Multiple Description Video Streaming over Overlay Networks," *Signal Processing: Image Communcation*, vol. 20, no. 1, pp. 39–60, Jan. 2005.

121. J. Apostolopoulos, "Error Resilient Video Compression via Multiple State Streams," *Proc. Int. Workshop on Very Low Bitrate Video Coding (VLBV'99), Kyoto, Japan*, pp. 168–171, Oct. 1999.

122. S. Ekmekci and T. Sikora, "Unbalanced Quantized Multi-State Video Coding: Potentials," *IEEE Picture Coding Symposium, San Francisco, USA*, Dec. 2004.

123. V. Goyal and J. Kovacevic, "Generalized Multiple Description Coding with Correlated Transforms," *IEEE Transactions on Information Theory*, vol. 47, no. 6, pp. 2199–2224, Sep. 2001.

124. I. Bajic and J. Woods, "Domain-based Multiple Description Coding of Images and Video," *Proc. of SPIE Conference on Visial Communicatins and Image Processing (VCIP), San Jose, USA*, pp. 124–135, Jan. 2002.

125. S. Lin and Y. Wang, "Analysis and Improvement of Multiple Description Motion Compensation Video Coding for Lossy Packet Networks," *Proc. IEEE Int. Conference on Image Processing (ICIP), Rochester, USA*, pp. 185–188, Sep. 2002.

126. T. Petrisor, C. Tillier, B. Pesquet-Popescu, and J.-C. Pesquet, "Redundant Multiresolution Analysis for Multiple Description Video Coding," *Proc. of the IEEE Int. Workshop on Multimedia Signal Processing (MMSP), Siena, Italy*, Sep. 2004.

127. I. Radulovic and P. Frossard, "Multiple Description Image Coding with Block-Coherent Redundant Dictionaries," *Proc. of Picture Coding Symposium, Hangzhou, China*, Apr. 2006.

128. J. Chakareski and B. Girod, "Server Diversity in Rate-Distortion Optimized Media Streaming," *Proc. IEEE Int. Conference on Image Processing (ICIP), Barcelona, Spain*, Sep. 2003.

129. J. Chakareski, E. Setton, Y. Liang, and B. Girod, "Video Streaming with Diversity," *Proc. IEEE Int. Conference on Multimedia and Expo, Baltimore, USA*, vol. 1, pp. 9–12, Jul. 2003.

130. J. Chakareski, S. Han, and B. Girod, "Layered Coding vs. Multiple Descriptions for Video Streaming over Multiple Paths," *Multimedia Systems, Springer, online journal publication: Digital Object Identifier (DOI) 10.1007/s00530-004-0162-3*, Jan. 2005.

131. T. Nguyen and A. Zakhor, "Distributed Video Streaming over the Internet," *Proc. of SPIE Conference on Multimedia Computing and Networking, San Jose, USA*, Jan. 2002.

132. D. Jurca and P. Frossard, "Media-Specific Rate Allocation in Multipath Networks," *Signal Processing Institute Technical Report - TR-ITS-2005.032*, Mar. 2006.

133. T. Nguyen and A. Zakhor, "Distributed Video Streaming with Forward Error Correction," *Proc. of Packet Video Workshop, Pittsburg, USA*, Apr. 2002.

134. ——, "Path Diversity with Forward Error Correction (PDF) System for Packet Switched Networks," *Proc. INFOCOM, San Francisco, USA*, vol. 3, pp. 663–672, Apr. 2003.

135. X. Zhu, E. Setton, and B. Girod, "Congestion-Distortion Optimized Video Transmission over Ad Hoc Networks," *Signal Processing: Image Communications*, no. 20, pp. 773–783, Sep. 2005.

136. E. Setton, T. Yoo, X. Zhu, A. Goldsmith, and B. Girod, "Cross-Layer Design of Ad Hoc Networks for Real-Time Video Streaming," *Wireless Communications Magazine*, vol. 12, no. 4, pp. 59–65, Aug. 2005.

137. S. Mao, S. Lin, S. Panwar, and Y. Wang, "A Multipath Video Streaming Testbed for Ad Hoc Networks," *Proc. of the Fall IEEE Vehicular Technology Conference, Orlando, Florida*, Oct. 2003.

138. W. Wei and A. Zakhor, "Multipath Unicast and Multicast Video Communication over Wireless Ad Hoc Networks," *Proc. of IEEE/ACM BroadNets*, pp. 496–505, Oct. 2004.

139. S. Deering, "Multicast Routing in a Datagram Internetwork," *Ph.D. thesis, Stanford University*, Dec. 1991.

140. X. Li, M. Ammar, and S. Paul, "Video Multicast over the Internet," *IEEE Networks*, vol. 13, no. 2, pp. 46–60, Mar. 1999.

141. J. Liu, B. Li, and Y.-Q. Zhang, "Adaptive Video Multicast over the Internet ," *IEEE Transactions on Multimedia*, vol. 10, no. 1, pp. 22–33, Jan. 2003.

142. S. McCanne, V. Jacobson, and M. Vetterli, "Receiver-Driven Layered Multicast," *Proc. of ACM SIGCOMM, Stanford, USA*, no. 117-130, Aug. 1996.

143. J. Apostolopoulos, W. Tan, and S. Wee, *Video Streaming: Concepts, Algorithms and Systems, in Handbook of Video Databases.* CRC Press, 2003.

144. R. Kermode, "Scoped Hybrid Automatic Repeat Request with Forward Error Correction," *Proc. of ACM SIGCOMM, Vancouver, Canada*, no. 278-289, Sep. 1998.

145. L. Rizzo and L. Vicisano, "A Reliable Multicast Data Distribution Protocol Based on Software FEC Techniques," *Proc. of HPCS, Chalkidiki, Greece*, Jun. 1997.

146. P. Chou, A. Mohr, A. Wang, and S. Mehrotra, "FEC and Pseudo-ARQ for Receiver-driven Layered Multicast of Audio and Video," *Proc. Data Compression Conference, Snowbird, USA*, pp. 440–449, Mar. 1999.

147. W. Tan and A. Zakhor, "Video Multicast using Layered FEC and Scalable Compression," *IEEE Transactions on Circuits and Systems on Video Technology*, vol. 11, no. 3, pp. 373–387, Mar. 2001.

148. "Akamai," *http://www.akamai.com, seen on Oct. 5 2006.*

149. "Limelight," *http://www.limelight.com, seen on Oct. 5 2006.*

150. "VitalStream," *http://www.vitalstream.com, seen on Oct. 5 2006.*

151. L. Kontothanassisy, R. Sitaramanz, J. Weinz, D. Hongz, R. Kleinberg, B. Mancusoz, D. Shawz, and D. Stodolsky, "A Transport Layer for Live Streaming in a Content Delivery Network," *Proc. of the IEEE*, vol. 92, no. 9, pp. 1408–1419, Sep. 2004.

152. L. Qiu, V. Padmanabhan, and G. Voelker, "On the Placement of Web Server Replicas," *Proc. INFOCOM, New York, USA*, pp. 1587–1596, Dec. 2001.

153. T. P.-C. Chen and T. Chen, "Second-Generation Error Concealment for Video Transport over Error Prone Channels," *Proc. Int. Conference on Image Processing (ICIP), Rochester, USA*, Sep. 2002.

154. J. Apostolopoulos, T. Wong, W. Tan, and S. Wee, "On Multiple Description Streaming Media Content Delivery Networks," *Proc. INFOCOM, New York, USA*, pp. 1736–1745, Jun. 2002.

155. M. Karlsson, C. Karamanolis, and M. Mahalingam, "A Framework for Evaluating Replica Placement Algorithms," *HPL Technical Report HPL-2002-219. available at http://www.hpl.hp.com/personal/Magnus_Karlsson/index.html.*

156. S. Banerjee, C. Kommareddy, K. Kar, B. Bhattacharjee, and S. Khuller, "Construction of an Efficient Overlay Multicast Infrastructure for Real-Time Applications," *Proc. INFOCOM, San Francisco, USA*, Jun. 2003.

157. J. Jannotti, D. Gifford, K. Johnson, M. Kaashoek, and J. O. Jr., "Overcast: Reliable Multicasting with an Overlay Network," *USENIX Symposium on Operation Systems Design and Implementation, San Diego, USA*, Oct. 2000.

158. Y. Chawathe, "Scattercast: an Adaptable Broadcast Distribution Framework," *Multimedia Systems*, vol. 9, no. 1, pp. 104–118, Jul. 2003.

159. D. Anderson and J. Kubiatowicz, "The Worldwide Computer," *Scientific American*, vol. 286, no. 3, pp. 28–35, Mar. 2002.

160. "Top Sourceforge Downloads," *http://sourceforge.net/top/.*

161. "BitTorrent Protocol Specification," *http://www.bittorrent.org/protocol.html, seen on Apr. 20 2007.*

162. D. Eastlake and P. Jones, "US Secure Hash Algorithm 1 (SHA-1)," *RFC 3174*, Sep. 2001.

163. S. Saroiu, P. Gummadi, and S. Gribble, "A Measurement Study of Peer-to-Peer File Sharing Systems," *Proc. Multimedia Computing and Networking (MMCN'02), San Jose, CA, USA*, Jan. 2002.

164. F. Bustamante and Y. Qiao, "Friendships that Last: Peer Lifespan and its Role in P2P Protocols," *Proc. Intl. Workshop on Web Content Caching and Distribution, Hawthorne, NY, USA*, Oct. 2003.

165. J. Pouwelse, P. Garbacki, D. Epema, and H. Sips, "The Bittorrent P2P Filesharing System: Measurements and Analysis," *4th International Workshop on Peer-to-Peer Systems (IPTPS), Ithaca, NY, USA*, Feb. 2005.

166. G. Neglia, G. Reina, H. Zhang, D. Towsley, A. Venkataramani, and J. Danaher, "Availability in BitTorrent Systems," *Proceedings of IEEE Infocom, Anchorage, AK, USA*, May 2007.

167. K. Sripanidkulchai, "The Popularity of Gnutella Queries and Its Implications on Scalability," *Technical report, Carnegie Mellon University*, Feb. 2001.

168. Y. Tian, D. Wu, and K.-W. Ng, "Modeling, Analysis and Improvement for Bittorrent-Like File Sharing Networks,," *Proc. IEEE INFOCOM, Barcelona, Spain*, Apr. 2006.

169. J. Wang, C. Yeo, V. Prabhakaran, and K. Ramchandran, "On the Role of Helpers in Peer-to-Peer File Download Systems: Design, Analysis and Simulation," *Proc. of the Sixth International Workshop on Peer-to-Peer Systems*, Feb. 2007.

170. S. Ratnasamy, P. Francis, M. Handley, R. Karp, and S. Schenker, "A Scalable Content-Addressable Network," *Proc. of ACM SIGCOMM, San Diego, USA*, pp. 161–172, Aug. 2001.

171. I. Stoica, R. Morris, D. Karger, F. Kaashoek, and H. Balakrishnan, "Chord: A Scalable Peer-To-Peer Lookup Service for Internet Applications," *Proc. of ACM SIGCOMM, San Diego, USA*, pp. 149–160, Aug. 2001.

172. J. Liebeherr, M. Nahas, and W. Si, "Application-layer Multicasting with Delaunay Triangulations Overlays," *IEEE Journal on Selected Areas in Communications*, vol. 20, no. 8, pp. 1472–1488, Oct. 2002.

173. M. Castro, P. Druschel, Y. Hu, and A. Rowstron, "Proximity Neighbor Selection in Tree-Based Structured Peer-to-Peer Overlays," *Technical report MSR-TR-2003-52*.

174. K. Hildrum, J. Kubiatowicz, S. Rao, and B. Zhao, "Distributed Object Location in a Dynamic Network ," *Theory of Computing Systems*, no. 37, pp. 405–440, Mar. 2004.

175. P. Maymounkov and D. Mazieres, "Kademlia: A peer-to-peer information system based on the xor metric," *In Proceedings of IPTPS02, Cambridge, MA, USA*, Mar. 2002.

176. M. Castro, M. Costa, and A. Rowstron, "Debunking Some Myths About Structured and Unstructured Overlays," *Proceedings of the 2nd Symposium on Networked Systems Design and Implementation, Boston, MA, USA*, May 2005.

177. S. Sheu, K. Hua, and W. Tavanapong, "Chaining: a Generalized Batching Technique for Video-on-Demand Systems," *Proc. IEEE Int. Conference Multimedia Computing and Systems, Ottawa, Canada*, pp. 110–117, Jun. 1997.

178. Y. Cui, B. Li, and K. Nahrstedt, "Layered Peer-to-Peer Streaming," *Proc. NOSSDAV'03, Monterey, USA*, pp. 162–171, Jun. 2003.

179. ——, "oStream: Asynchronous Streaming Multicast in Application-Layer Overlay Networks," *IEEE Journal on Selected Areas in Communications*, vol. 22, no. 1, Jan. 2004.

180. Z. Xiang, Q. Zhang, W. Zhu, Z. Zhang, and Y.-Q. Zhang, "Peer-to-Peer Based Multimedia Distribution Service," *IEEE Transactions on Multimedia*, vol. 6, no. 2, pp. 343–355, Apr. 2004.

181. X. Xu, Y. Wang, S. Panwar, and K. Ross, "A Peer-to-Peer Video-on-Demand System using Multiple Description Coding and Server Diversity," *Proc. IEEE Int. Conference on Image Processing (ICIP), Singapore*, vol. 3, pp. 1759–1762, Oct. 2004.

182. Y. Chu, S. Rao, S. Seshan, and H. Zhang, "A Case for End System Multicast," *IEEE Journal on Selected Areas in Communications*, vol. 20, no. 8, pp. 1456–1471, Oct. 2002.

183. S. Banerjee, B. Bhattacharjee, and C. Kommareddy, "Scalable Application Layer Multicast," *Proc. ACM SIGCOMM, Pittsburgh, USA*, pp. 205–217, Aug. 2002.

184. D. Tran, K. Hua, and T. Do, "ZIGZAG: An Efficient Peer-to-Peer Scheme for Media Streaming," *Proc. IEEE INFOCOM, San Francisco, USA*, vol. 2, pp. 1283–1292, Mar. 2003.

185. Y. Chu, A. Ganjam, T. Ng, S. Rao, K. Sripanidkulchai, J. Zhan, and H. Zhang, "Early Experience with an Internet Broadcast System Based on Overlay Multicast," *Proc. USENIX Annual Technical Conference, Boston, MA, USA*, pp. 1283–1292, Jun. 2004.

186. Y. Zhu, B. Li, and J. Guo, "Multicast with Network Coding in Application-Layer Overlay Networks," *IEEE Journal on Selected Areas in Communications*, vol. 1, no. 22, pp. 107–120, Jan. 2004.

187. X. Zhang, J. Liu, B. Li, and T.-S. P. Yum, "DONet/CoolStreaming: A Data-driven Overlay Network for Live Media Streaming," *Proc. IEEE Infocom, Miami, USA*, Feb. 2005.

188. M. Zhang, J.-G. Luo, L. Zhao, and S.-Q. Yang, "A Peer-to-Peer Network for Live Media Streaming using a Push-Pull Approach," *Proc. ACM Int. Conference on Multimedia*, pp. 287–290, Nov. 2005.

189. ——, "Large-Scale Live Media Streaming over Peer-to-Peer Networks through Global Internet," *Proc. ACM Int. Conference on Multimedia, P2PMMS Workshop*, pp. 21–28, Nov. 2005.

190. B. Ford, P. Sisuresh, and D. Kegel, "Peer-to-Peer Communication across Network Address Translators," *Proc. USENIX Annual Technical Conference, Anaheim, CA, USA*, pp. 179–192, Apr. 2005.

191. A. Biggadike, D. Ferullo, G. Wilson, and A. Perrig, "NATBLASTER: Establishing TCP Connections Between Hosts behind NATs," *Proc. ACM SIGCOMM, Asia Workshop, Beijing, China*, Apr. 2005.

192. J. Rosenberg, J. Weinberger, C. Huitema, and R. Mahy, "STUN - Simple Traversal of User Datagram Protocol (UDP) through Network Address Translators (NATs), RFC 3489," Mar. 2003.

193. J. Rosenberg, C. Huitema, and R. Mahy, "Traversal using Relay NAT (TURN), Internet Draft," Oct. 2003.

194. J. Rosenberg, "Interactive Connectivity Establishment (ICE): a Methodology for Network Address Translator (NAT) Traversal for Multimedia Session Establishment Protocols, Internet Draft," Feb. 2004.

195. M. Bansal and A. Zakhor, "Path Diversity for Overlay Multicast Streaming," *Proc. Packet Video Worshop, Irvine, CA, USA*, Dec. 2004.

196. V. Padmanabhan, H. Wang, and P. Chou, "Resilient Peer-to-Peer Streaming," *IEEE Int. Conference on Network Protocols, Atlanta, USA*, Nov. 2003.

197. V. Padmanabhan, H. Wang, P. Chou, and K. Sripanidkulchai, "Distributing Streaming Media Content Using Cooperative Networking," *Proc. NOSSDAV'02, Miami, USA*, May 2002.

198. E. Setton, X. Zhu, and B. Girod, "Minimizing Distortion for Multipath Video Streaming over Ad Hoc Networks," *Proc. Int. Conference on Image Processing (ICIP), Singapore*, vol. 3, pp. 1751–1754, Oct. 2004.

199. E. Setton, J. Noh, and B. Girod, "Rate-Distortion Optimized Video Peer-to-Peer Multicast Streaming," *Proc. of the ACM workshop on Advances in peer-to-peer multimedia streaming P2PMMS'05 , Singapore*, pp. 39–45, Nov. 2005.

200. "The Network Simulator - ns-2," *www.isi.edu/nsnam/ns/*.

201. E. Setton and B. Girod, "Congestion-Distortion Optimized Scheduling of Video," *Multimedia Signal Processing Workshop (MMSP), Siena, Italy*, pp. 99–102, Oct. 2004.

202. E. Setton, X. Zhu, and B. Girod, "Congestion-Optimized Scheduling of Video over Wireless Ad Hoc Networks," *Proc. Int. Symposium on Circuits and Systems (ISCAS), Kobe, Japan*, vol. 4, pp. 3531–3534, May 2005.

203. A. Mukherjee, "On the Dynamics and Significance of Low Frequency Components of Internet Load," *Internetworking: Research and Experience*, vol. 5, pp. 163–205, Dec. 1994.

204. M. Kalman and B. Girod, "Modeling the Delays of Successively-Transmitted Internet Packets," *Proc. Int. Conference on Multimedia and Expo (ICME), Taipei, Taiwan*, Jul. 2004.

205. A. Leon-Garcia, *Probability and Random Processes for Electrical Engineering.* MA: Addison-Wesley, 1994.

206. J. Strauss, D. Katabi, and F. Kaashoek, "A Measurement Study of Available Bandwidth Estimation Tools," *Proc. of the 3rd ACM SIGCOMM Conference on Internet Measurement, Miami Beach, CA, USA*, pp. 39–44, Oct. 2003.

207. R. Zhang-Shen and N. McKeown, "Designing a Predictable Internet Backbone with Valiant Load-Balancing," *Thirteenth International Workshop on Quality of Service (IWQoS 2005), Passau, Germany*, pp. 174–188, Jun. 2005.

208. "PlanetLab," *http://www.planet-lab.org*, seen on Apr. 12 2007.

209. P. Baccichet, J. Noh, E. Setton, and B. Girod, "Content-Aware P2P Video Streaming With Low Latency," *Proc. IEEE Int. Conference on Multimedia and Expo (ICME), Beijing, China, to appear*, Jul. 2007.

210. K. Sripanidkulchai, A. Ganjam, B. Maggs, and H. Zhang, "The Feasibility of Supporting LargeScale Live Streaming Applications with Dynamic Application EndPoints," *Proc. SIGCOMM'04, Portland, USA*, Aug. 2004.

211. E. Setton, J. Noh, and B. Girod, "Low Latency Video Sreaming over Peer-to-Peer Networks," *Proc. IEEE Int. Conference on Multimedia and Expo (ICME), Toronto, Canada*, pp. 569–572, Jul. 2006.

212. J. Chakareski and B. Girod, "Computing Rate-Distortion Optimized Policies for Streaming Media with Rich Acknowledgements," *Proc. IEEE Data Compression Conference, Snowbird, USA*, pp. 202–211, Apr. 2004.

213. E. Setton, P. Baccichet, and B. Girod, "Peer-to-Peer Live Multicast: A Video Perspective," *Proc. of the IEEE, submitted*.

214. K. Stuhlmüller, *Modeling and Optimization of Video Transmission Systems,* Ph.D. Dissertation, University of Erlangen, 2000.

Index

ACK, 10, 47–50, 90
ADSL, 78
Akamai, 13
application layer, 11, 17, 18, 86
ARQ, *see* automatic repeat request
ATM, 17
automatic repeat request, 10, 19, 48,
    51, 52, 56–59, 61

best-effort, 8
bottleneck link, 19, 24, 28, 29, 34–36,
    40, 51, 52, 56, 61, 92, 115
bottleneck queue, 31–38, 40, 42, 45, 46,
    51, 56, 61, 89, 120
broadband, 8
broadcast, 14

CAN, 16
CAVLC, 118
Chord, 16
CIF, 21, 26, 27, 121, 123, 125, 127, 129,
    131
client-server, *see* server-client
coding
    channel coding, 9
    coding dependency, 118
    coding structure, 19, 21, 24, 28, 30,
        34, 37, 41, 44, 47, 91, 92, 94, 96,
        97, 102, 106–108, 117, 118, 122,
        124, 126, 128, 130, 132
    entropy coding, 5, 6, 118
    intra-coding, 5, 6, 9, 20, 21
    layered coding, 9–11, 13, 18, 34, 116,
        117

motion-compensated, 5–7, 21
multiple description coding, 12, 18,
    114
single-layer, 11, 12, 18
VBR, 28
coding structure, 20, 21, 38, 50, 51, 91,
    94, 95, 117
congestion control, 8, 11, 33
content delivery network, 1, 13, 78
content-adaptive, 12, 114
content-aware, *see* content-adaptive
content-oblivious, 19, 90, 101, 106–108
control overhead, 64, 74, 79–81, 86, 103,
    104, 116
convergence, 10, 41
convex, 24, 41
convolution, 34
CPU, 90

data-driven, 16
deadline
    decoding deadline, 29, 38, 40, 106
    playout deadline, 29–33, 38, 42, 47,
        48, 50–54, 56–59, 61, 88, 92, 96,
        97, 102, 106, 107
degree, 78, 85
delay
    end-to-end delay, 10, 19, 20, 24,
        33–36, 48, 50, 51, 54, 55, 60, 89,
        96, 111, 116
    propagation delay, 34, 36, 40, 47, 50,
        51, 78
    startup delay, 1, 8, 17, 116
deployment, 14, 63, 116

Printed in the United States of America.